Best Of Intentions
A Story of
Government Spies and SDI

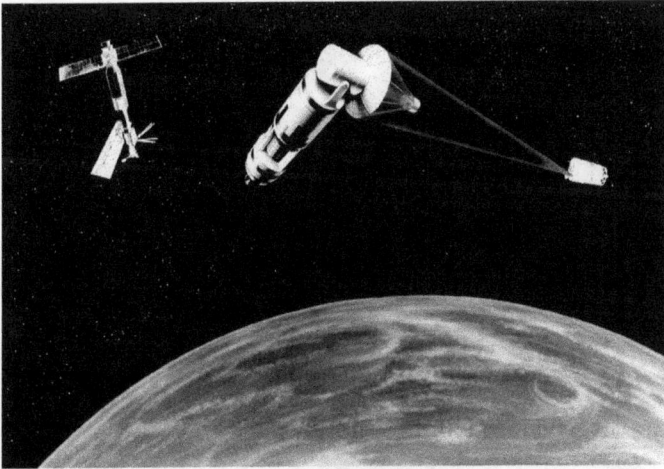

Mike Hughes

C2C Publications

Other Books by Mike Hughes include:

The Northwest Dive Guide by Harbour Publishing 2009

The North American Dive Guide

To Kill A Diver. A Murder Mystery

Whoops Airlines Enhanced. Cartoon Book

Whoops Divers Guide. Cartoon Book

Although I first wrote this book some 15 years ago, many parts of the SDI Initiative are still being worked on, albeit different names.

About the Author:
Mike Hughes graduated as a marine Biologist from San Francisco State University. He spent over 8 years as a Russian and Spanish interpreter for Pan American World Airways. He flew to Moscow when the Soviet Union was still in full force, the KGB monitored foreigner activities, Russian Rubles were worth $1.35 at Russian State Banks, but sold on the black market in Frankfurt, Germany for a mere 35 cents each. The Berlin Wall came down less than ten years later.

This Book Is Dedicated Posthumously To My Mother
Sandra Joy Adams

BEST OF INTENTIONS

CHAPTER 1

Shimmering waves of heated air hovered above the newly paved black tarmac. Looking out his window, Paul watched the pavement turn into a molten black sea of ooze. He could barely discern the ripples of energy being generated at the borders where tar met with, and often times, overlapped cement. The waves formed a barrier; a warning to those who would otherwise cross the boundary, that this pseudo La Brae tar pit, would devour all hapless victims who strayed across its path. His short sleeve shirt began to show signs of crescent shaped sweat stains. He tapped the round face of the digital thermometer again. It maintained the reading of 102.75 degrees. "As if .75 makes a difference." Alone in the office he often talked out loud to himself. He took out his old red Boy Scout necktie that he had made into handkerchief. The blue and white emblem of Spirit Lake and Mount ST. Helen had almost completely rubbed off. Since the May 1980 eruption the Boy Scout camp he once stayed at was buried under tons of silica. He wondered if they would ever try to rebuild the camp. He knew he would never forget Spirit Lake. It was there that he and his eleven year old best friend Stevie, stole two six packs of soda pop from a near by campsite. The pop was ice cold, just lying in the stream. The two of them picked up the pop and ran towards the lake. Unfortunately, someone spotted them and the chase was on. As juvenile delinquents, he and Stevie spent over an hour hiding inside upside down canoes stacked on a rack near the water's edge. They were scared to death and both of them knew, that if caught, they would be kicked out of the scouts, or even worse, have another talk with their parents. But none of their pursuers ever found their hiding spot. The pop was still cold by the time they made it back to their own camp. He wished he had a cold can of pop right now.

He could still see the faint outline on the handkerchief where the Boy Scout symbol was imprinted. He wiped off the perspiration that formed on his forehead and upper lip. His eyes took on a glassy sheen. His chest felt tight. His throat was dry and parched.

"I've got to get some air in here." He went over to the window and gripped the old brass handles. The locks had been painted over with white enamel one too many times. They were impossible to disengage; one of the few things in this house/converted office center that hadn't been upgraded. The caked layers of paint finally cracked; gave way, and up slid the pane of glass. "Oh, no," he realized he had made a dreadful mistake, but it was too late. A heat wave with the strong smell of tar swept into his office. There was no escape. He accepted his fate. His lungs began to burn as he peered out the window in defiance. Across the street he gazed at his burgeoning empire. He beamed with pride as he gazed at a large two story flat brown colored building that still looked fairly new compared to the surrounding structure in the industrial park. It would have been inconceivable for him to think that, all this could be destroyed, in less time than a blink of an eye.

The main lights were off at the warehouse and the adjacent employees parking lot was void of cars. Inside, an air conditioner kept the manufacturing facility cooled to a nice 68 degrees. As President and owner of Crelco Industries, he could afford an installed air conditioner in his office, but his wife in her infinite wisdom talked him out of it. She showed him a magazine article on catching colds and that air conditioners were bad for one's health. He removed his air conditioner to appease her. Now, as he felt a trickle of sweat snake down the nape of his neck, he swore he'd never read one of those yuppie trend articles again.

Paul was in his mid-forties, in good health, and his hair had only a touch of gray near his temple. He stood by the window daydreaming about how large his company would become, until the--Ok--wave from the overweight security guard woke him up. The two of them mutually responded with hand gestures on many a night. A sort of ritual they abided by when he was working late. He waved back, and strode towards his CEO comfort room: a small cubicle walled off, and stuffed in the corner of his office. The sink and toilet were standard original fixtures when a farming family first built the house. Even with new linoleum and fresh paint, he detected the faint smell of urine emanating from underlying floorboards, but he was content with his surroundings for the time being. This building would be bulldozed and replaced during the next fiscal year.

"Maybe some cold water on my face would help."

Clarence Omalery, the sedentary security guard whose stomach was the only part of him that worked full time, had just set his magazine down and was reaching for his thermos when he happened to see Paul, the President of Crelco Industries, looking across the street at him. He waved his pudgy fingers at the boss. "Jesus, that was close." Timing was crucial in his line of work. Normally he checked around the job site before he began his relaxed shift, or at least he imagined he did, but tonight he forgot, or at least he thought he did. He walked around the building twice already. He didn't check to see if the doors were locked. He merely surveyed the area and headed back to his lookout post. He looked at his watch. It had been two hours since he last made his rounds. He wasn't looking forward to getting tar on his new pair of working boots. The job was so monotonous. Tonight, he couldn't wait to peek inside the current edition of sports illustrated. A slightly abused swimsuit edition packed with women twice as thin as his wife had ever been, and women that probably lusted for men four times as trim as he was, but that didn't put a damper on his imagination. But if the boss was watching with his window open, it was time for him to grab a cup of steaming black coffee, then make the rounds. Good easy jobs were hard to come by, he thought a he checked his shoelaces.

After his stint in Korea, the last thing Clarence wanted to see was action. His shrapnel scared legs attested, to his close encounter with death. Just a routine patrol that sent a scrawny red hair, pink eyed, kid flying through the air. An incoming mortar shell killed two of his friends. He was lucky and woke up on a plane bound for the States. PGI, Patrol Guards Incorporated, knew his sentiment too, that's why he always got such assignments. When asked by his coworkers what he'd do if approached by thieves, he would smile and gesture by pulling out his black, long handled, metal flashlight. Then on cue, someone would remark: "So you can guide them in the dark." To this well used line the rest of his cohorts would laugh at him. He didn't mind it really, most of them were half his age with half his commitments and they hadn't yet faced what he'd experienced. Playing superman with thieves was suicide as far as he was concerned.

He had a family to think about and Colleta his wife made doubly sure he didn't forget it.

His motto was, anyone not related by blood, he judged unfamiliar. Anyone unfamiliar, he judged suspicious. Anything suspicious he reported to the police. That was his job; call the police. He figured as long as guard dogs couldn't dial 911 or talk, his job was secure. The rest of the time he read and drank coffee. He took a sip of the hot black coffee from his favorite unwashed cup. On the side of the cup under layers of coffee stains read the inscription 'World's Greatest Dad.' It was his wife's way of further reminding him where his duties rested. Looking up from his cup he noticed the boss was gone. He hoped Dr. Crellin, the boss, would be leaving soon, then the shift would go by as slow and uneventful as all the other post season football nights.

Clarence's teeth for some reason felt loose. He spent a few moments rechecking his dental bridge. He didn't notice the two men dressed in American-French cut two piece business suits sitting at the far end of the street in a rented black BMW. The two out of towners would have preferred one hundred percent wool suits tailored in England, but they wore the western mix blend, common gray, as the local customs dictated, to fit in. They looked just like two ordinary mid-level executives only they were not your typical corporate raiders.

"That guard is worthless," one of the men remarked.

"Too bad he doesn't get paid by the pound."

"They've got their priorities all mixed up. They pay Chairman's of the Board millions of dollars to screw the workers and sell out the corporation, but they pay minimum wage to the guy whose guarding the company's assets. It makes no sense at all!"

"You're right about that."

"I'm glad we get to help accelerate their demise."

The tightly sealed tinted windows helped obscure their faces, but they could have used some ventilation. If only your face wasn't so Ukrainian looking, Dave thought, scrutinizing his partner, Carl's, profile. Both men had assumed North American names. Carl's red Ukrainian colored skin, his slicked back silver hair, and his hazel-gray eyes were clearly non-typical in America. Dave wondered how Carl had ever gotten so far in the old organization sometimes, but he knew. The man was second cousin of someone influential in the old Party. How else did anyone get ahead? He was jealous and upset that his own family had been so non-party oriented. Yes, they could now say they had been right all along. But what benefits did that give them? It meant he had an uphill battle from the very start. Dave felt he surely looked like a typical San Franciscan. Wind tossed Brown hair, brown eyes, slightly tanned, and a physique somewhere between body builder and surfer-athlete. He had been selected for this assignment from the very beginning. He could pass himself off as any nationality, and in the past he did just that. And look at his partner. The least Carl could have done was trim his bristling eyebrows. The man looked like Breshnev reincarnated. Maybe he was being too critical. Of course, being critical was easy for a hardened Muscovite. Still, Dave was aware that any unusual look was common in California. In fact, most probably, his superior perhaps, fit in better than he did. Maybe that's why he chose to look the very image of the old Rodina. What a screwy, yet, marvelous place is this America.

On the way here, they passed by several BMW's. In this part of town BMW's were more common than Fords in Detroit, but the two agents didn't dare roll down the dark tinted widows for fear of being observed. In downtown San Francisco the two of them might appear as just another gay couple discussing day to day family matters, but two business men silently dying of heat prostration was highly suspicious. So if they had to sweat, then it was better to do it as inconspicuously as possible. Sitting in the passenger seat, Dave turned his attention to the car's interior. He could never get over how well it was designed. There were buttons and dials galore, and a smooth handling stick shift. He had used this model many times in the past. With its speed and agility, the old agency preferred this car for this city terrain. Too bad he didn't have time to steal it and ship it home to Russia. Foreign car sales with no questions asked, was a thriving industry back home. He had friends who could ship it via the Port of Seattle, Washington for next to nothing and it could be unloaded and driving down the dirt roads of Vladivostock within a few days.

"What's that fat oaf doing now?" Carl jerked his head up, pointing at the guard.

Everything had been planned down to the last detail, and now, Bozo, the overweight security guard was changing his nightly routine. They watched anxiously as Clarence walked behind the far side of the building.

"He must have gotten spooked when he saw his boss."

Dave reached over to turn up the air conditioner, but remembered with the motor off, it could drain the battery. Then how would they get away? Always have an escape route. No Errors. The entrenched KGB mottoes raced through his mind. Out of the corner of his eye, Carl watched his partner's motions. He had been thinking the same thing. He could feel his own perspiration congealing under his shirt.

"We'll just have to wait a little longer and hope that we don't fry like Piroskis in the mean time," said Carl.

After some fifteen minutes Clarence finally returned to his guardhouse. "That's our cue," snapped Carl. The two figures got out of the car and felt the rush of hot foul air.

"Lock it."

"I did." came Dave's monotone reply. Carl made this statement every time they got out of a car. He never could get used to California and held a degree of distrust for all and anyone since his last assignment on the east coast. However, the degree of distrust was still less here than when they were home in Moscow, but that was to be expected. With all the reforms and the new lower profile of the KGB, came the new unavoidable crime wave.

Now everyone in Moscow seemed to have their hands desperately mounting searches for ulterior avenues to self-help. If things got worse, he just might decide to stay in America.

"You ready?" Dave slapped the black nylon bag he was carrying with his free hand. Dave never spoke much during a mission. If conversation was desired, he'd use sign language.

"Lets go." The two men walked in the opposite direction of Crelco Industries, turned down the first driveway they came to, and headed behind an adjacent building.

A galvanized metal chain fence separated the two properties. It took but seconds for the two former amateur athletes to reach the other side. One at a time they climbed over the fence so they could gently hand over the bag. By the time Dave, the back-up man, hit the pavement, Carl was already running for the back door's loading ramp. Up he went at full speed. At the same time he reached into his pocket for a key. What a slick mission he thought. No prying doors or anything. The entire operation had been handed to him on a silver platter. This was definitely not the usual scenario, which meant even more, that the people in control wanted this to go exactly as planned. It made him wonder why such a small upstart company commanded so much attention from his superiors. He decided that the success of this mission could only lead to his further advancement. Funny he thought, most men advanced by constructive endeavors. His achievements in rank were marked by wholesale destruction. God he enjoyed his work! He inserted the key and the back door unlocked. A cool breeze that smelled of metal and acid waited over him and Dave who presently stood beside him catching his breath. If the alarm was going to go off, it would have to be now or never. He heard nothing. He smiled at Dave. The worst part was over; the alarm had been bypassed as promised. They entered single file. Once inside the lighted interior, Dave closed the door while Carl unzipped the bag and spread it open so he could view the contents. While he stared in admiration at his goodies, he inhaled their coffee-caramel candy fragrance and his stomach began to grumble. What a beautiful site they were. His comrade looked at him and grinned. The feeling was mutual. Separated by a thin nylon cover from the cold cement floor, lay six newly developed high-density explosives. Basically a microchip and a blasting cap on a piece of plastic explosive, they left no discernible traces. Better yet, they were remote control activated.

After a moment of respect and admiration, he picked up the contents and went to work. Dave, second in command, watched the door. It was suppose to be a piece of cake, but if that bumbling oaf Clarence decided to make another round, they would have to take him out, if only for his own safety. Their orders stated no one killed or injured, but that wasn't always possible. Even routine operations could ask for the impossible; their orders were very explicit.

Carl set about his task with amazing speed. Their information had been precise down to the last detail. The charges were planted in easy to reach recesses. The strategic importance of the locations had been made very clear. The ensuing event had to look natural. Like a grain elevator filled with volatile dust particles, chemicals routinely used in manufacturing processes would inevitably get the blame. Three minutes later he was racing back to the door. Not a word spoken: None were needed. With neither time to look around or behind, out the back door and over the fence they bolted. As they approached the corner of the building, they slowed down, straightened their ties and sauntered towards their car, but the car was gone. Both men stared at the fragments of glass littering the street next to where the car had once been parked. Amused by the incident, Carl stated, "Break My Window". Dave appeared puzzled by the statement. "I heard it's a nick name for BMW," Carl quickly added. With just under five minutes of curbside downtime, someone had stolen the car.

"Well, assign me to a former collective farm." Carl said nothing further nor showed any sign of emotion. He just started walking down the street away from the immediate area.

"We could have used the air conditioner after all," Dave said as they strolled down the street.

"The battery would have drained," Carl reminded him.

"Yes, but the car would still be there, instead of stolen." Carl smiled and shrugged his shoulders. He continued walking on in silence. Two blocks away he spotted the sign of a Friday's restaurant. The parking lot was filled with cars. From across the street they spotted a field of BMW'S. Having acquired a true capitalistic taste for the finer things in life, both men paid special attention to a lone, maroon colored,

Jaguar. Although for their purposes, the fifty-eight classic was just a little too conspicuous. They smiled at one another as if they read each other's thoughts, and then headed across the street.

"Thieves and ex-party members are everywhere." Ex-driver, Carl, spoke out as were about halfway across the intersection. "Shall we stop for a vodka before we drive home?"

"Da Comrade, but I've never heard you so openly comment on the authority before." Carl looked sternly at him then broke into a genuine smile.

"How about this one? Where I come from, there is an old joke, "What do you call a collective farm filled with intelligent children, but with their parents not party members?" Dave kept silent, the connotation hit too close to home. "Field of Dreams".

Carl chuckled for a moment then abruptly stopped. "I ran away very young, my aunt in

Moscow used to sleep with a party member." Dave realized they shared common ground after all. There was little left for comment. The two somber businessmen headed for the other curb and turned in the direction of the restaurant entrance.

Inside, they felt assailed by hazy smoke and loud modern music. Most of the patrons wore business attire similar to their own. These happy hour regulars were not the brains behind Silicon Valley, but the essential managers and marketing people that assured the success for the constantly burgeoning computer firms. The two KGB operatives blended in with the crowd better than they had anticipated.

"Two vodka's and coke," Carl told the bartender. "Rum may be the traditional mix with coke, but I've spent more than enough share of my time in Cuba. Even the thought of rum reminds me of Cuba, and the thought of that backwards Island, leaves a bad taste in anyone's mouth."

"You sound like it was paradise before the revolution." Dave countered.

"Maybe not for the locals, but at least for the tourists. Too bad it always has to be one group or another. Otherwise, Cuba might have been left unspoiled." With drinks in hand, they sat on some nearby stools.

"In a place like this," Carl continued, the only time you don't have a drink in your hand is when you were leaving. That's how you blend in; that's how the place makes money. Being a single's pick-up spot just makes business that much better. I would like to own just such an establishment someday. What do you think?"

"I think you get too easily side tracked." Dave then saw a couple of very attractive women looking their way. He thought California was truly paradise. But right now, he still had a mission to fulfill.

Carl gradually pulled a small thin plastic case out of his pocket. Dave's eyes focused on the shiny black object. Carl flicked it open to reveal a small grid of diodes with an on/off button. Six diodes emitted a bright red light.

"You care to hear a little something with cannons? This music suck." Carl said.

A contorted grin appeared on his face.

"You mean 'sucks'," Dave corrected him. He realized he'd gone too far when he saw the sinister grin on Carl's face, the same grin he'd seen countless other times before. Although Dave was about as ruthless as they came, at times like these, he looked right into his partner's eyes and felt a tinge of fear. Capable of anything, this former USSR psychopath enjoyed life only when deep in focus with his twisted line of work. Carl would go far in the new KGB and would go even farther with his latest employer. Their line of work would always be in demand, although more subtle in delivery, even if America and Russia became the best of allies. Great Job security!.

"This place is much too quiet." Dave replied. Carl depressed the button. The diode lights blinked off. A far off "whomp" could be heard; almost felt deep in their chests. It could have been the backfire of a car, but it wasn't.

"A little anticlimactic wouldn't you say?" Carl sighed. "No loud boom, no cries of anguish, nothing." The word is anticlimactic Dave thought, but he did not dare correct his superior again. The man should stick to simple words.

"Well yes, za zdarovaya anyway." Dave raised his glass then took a sip. With the operation completed, they would wait for most of the sirens to pass by, then leave discreetly. Carl took note of a tall slinky blonde standing by the counter. He loved blondes, especially slinky blondes. Particularly ones that wore shirt tops that barely covered their chests and revealed inches of sensuous skin. A light blue bra beneath a white see-through blouse delivered the final punch that brought down his guard. For a split instance in time, he thought about screwing his orders and pledging his life to her. It wouldn't have been the first time he disobeyed orders, and this is precisely why he was paired up with this slightly younger, more by the book guy in the first place. The trip back to their safe house was going to be even gloomier after being in a place like this.

Clarence lost his grip and his freshly poured cup of coffee shot out of his hands as the explosion. Hot coffee landed on his pants. The flesh on his legs peeled away from his flesh and clung instead to the cotton fibers of his pants. He screamed in pain and tried to stand up but was knocked to the ground as a giant fireball belched out of the building and engulfed the structure in flames. Black soot dusted everything around him. He coughed up dark colored mucus. His lungs and throat burned from the inhaled debris.

Half stunned and rising to his feet, he picked up the phone to call the fire department. It was just like Korea. Just like reliving an episode better left in history, he felt himself slip back into combat mode. He had orders to follow and he felt immune to further danger. The line was dead. He looked out the booth and saw where the phone line once ran from the booth to the burning building, a charred cord remained. Compelled to sound out an alarm, he stampeded towards the street. Halfway across the street, he saw Mr. Crellin, present owner of the towering inferno, coming out of the office complex.

"How bad is it?" Paul asked between coughs. His face was ash white. Paul looked as if he was ready to go into shock. He didn't hear Clarence answer back. He didn't even notice Clarence gallop past him as he watched in disbelief as the building was transformed into a gutted cinder block. He felt the sudden urge to throw up as he watched his empire turn to ashes. He calculated six months before he'd be back in operation, but by then, the inroads by his competition would devastate his share of the market.

As the smoke from the burning debris rose and mixed with the upper air currents, a dark cloud formed over his head. He coughed again. It didn't hurt his throat as much this time. He tried to see through the smoggy mass floating above him. He expected this too to pass. The setting sun was blotted out; a temporary inconvenience. He didn't recognize it for the ominous warning that it was meant to be.

Chapter 2

"Where is that son of a bitch," Paul yelled out as he made his way down the hall.

"Police came by and they said they couldn't find him." Clarence Omalery replied.

He was practically running, trying to keep up with Paul. They were both marched down the hall of the annex building; the only structure presently intact and remaining of Crelco Industries. Paul opened the door and entered the office room of his accountant Leonard Goldsmith. Goldsmith wasn't in his office as expected. The phone on the desk rang. Paul pressed a button and switched on the speaker.

"Yes."

"Dr. Crellin?" came the soft voice of his secretary. "The FBI called back. They say Leonard Goldsmith doesn't exist, so he can't be kidnapped."

"That's impossible, Ann."

"You want me to call the insurance company again?"

"Yes. . . And this time ask to speak to someone way up."

"Yes, Dr. Crellin." The phone clicked off. Paul looked down on the contents lying on the desk. There had to be someone named Leonard Goldsmith. His writings, notes, and personal effects were all over the room. Company reports occupied the top of the desk. Some were open and marked with red ink. Leonard might have just stepped out for a drink of water. A picture of his family lay on the desk. A picture of his dog sat on the bookshelf. Abruptly, he realized, there was no picture of Leonard. Paul went around and pulled open the top desk drawer. A few pens, pencils, and company stationary items lined the drawer. There was nothing to suggest whom the man that worked in this office looked like.

Assorted books and papers cluttered the bookshelves, but nothing to show whom the man was other than his signature. Someone glancing in the once would see a busy work setting. The lack of occupancy wouldn't raise an eyebrow of suspicion. Leonard left for good. But how long ago? Damn him! Paul came in wanting to strangle the greasy hair bastard with his bare hands. He would start by breaking Leonard's eyeglasses and making him eat them if he didn't tell him what happened to the insurance money.

"Mr. Reems with the insurance on line two," Ann's voice came out over the phone's speaker. Paul pushed the button.

"Mr. Reems, any update?"

"I'm afraid it's bad news."

"Go on."

"Apparently, you canceled your insurance premiums four months ago."

"Who authorized the cancellation?" Inside Paul knew that's when Leonard took over accounting.

"It says here, we quite receiving the payments and so we automatically discontinued the policy. That's odd because the banks require insurance to cover the loan."

"I paid the bank loan off a year ago." Paul said as his heart began to beat faster.

"Oh, I'm sorry to hear that. Ah, but we sent several notices. We never received a reply. I've got the dates posted right here the days the letters were sent. We do it automatically. We keep good track of all our clients, and we do everything we can to keep them for life. I'm sorry to hear about your fire, but there's not much we can do."

"Thank you Mr. Reems." Paul shut the speaker off and looked at nothing in particular. With fake credentials, someone came to work and within months literally destroys everything. It was actually a two step process.. Leonard discontinued paying the fire insurance premiums without Paul's consent. Then conveniently, the manufacturing plant burns down to the ground wiping out everything save the office space across the street; an expensive lesson. Too much trust in the hands of one employee cost him his business, his lifestyle, and the world, as he knew it. A corporate raider couldn't have left him feeling more used and abused. He had to somehow find a way to give his business a second chance. But right now every day his company sat idle in ashes cost him a slice of his previous market share and made it just that much harder to get back in business. He started to doubt whether a second chance was even possible.

CHAPTER 3

Paul sat on a brand new sofa in a newly remodeled office. The cushion squeaked every time he shifted his weight. The squeaking noise was wearing on his patience, which made him shift his weight even more. The couch needed to be broken in, and his backside was beginning to ache. The room looked and smelled of fresh paint and new furnishings, the way his new office should have looked like had he been able to keep his own company. The acidic odors swirled in the air, went into his lungs and burned the cell lining, but these were mild discomforts; he hated the waiting most of all. At times like these he wished he'd brought a book, but reading a novel didn't seem appropriate prior to such an important meeting. The next few hours could either mean a job and prosperity, or another month without income and putting off another mortgage payment?

Trying to keep busy he scrutinized the pictures that hung in various arrangements on the walls. Cows grazing in the fields seemed to be the predominant theme. They were gaudy imitations of country scenes. All they needed were nuclear energy plants painted in the distance to make the scene complete. He had nothing against country scenes, they just reminded him of the ones folks gave away at gas stations, when people filled their gas tank up when he was a small boy. Maybe they're not gaudy or simplistic he thought. Maybe, they're just artifacts of nebulous mass media at its' best.

He stood up, gazed out the large window making up almost the entire length of the right hand wall, and studied a distant field. There, the ground stages of yet another building were underway. Years ago cows grazed in that field. The cows were all gone. They only remained in the paintings. An image of golden arches flashed through his mind.

After a while, he checked his watch. Fifty minutes had passed since he first entered the room with no sign of anyone save a middle-aged secretary named Ruth Kamakura. Her wide shoulders made her appear short. Sparse, close-cut, black hair and bright ruby red lipstick either balanced out her proportions or gave her a bigger than life image.

"Would you like something to drink, Dr. Crellin?" she asked, but she didn't look like she really meant it. She touched her hair to see if everything was in place. The perm was still holding she decided.

"No thanks."

"I'm sorry for the delay," she said. She held a magazine in her left hand. Her index finger pressed firmly against the spot where she temporarily stopped reading.

She appeared anxious to leave him alone and resume the article. If the intent was to down play the impending dialogue, then those in charge were doing a real good job.

They had him pegged, he thought. They knew what he wanted and they wanted him to know that they knew. Disgusted, he let out a deep sigh. Ten years in Silicon Valley and he was still trying to secure a job. His neck, no longer able to hold up its heavy burden, let his cerebral mass sag as he watched the sun filter into the room. Tiny particles of dust thrown upwards by the air currents gleamed under the sun's rays, not dust particles he decided, but the by-product of a newly installed carpet. In his opinion, each particle represented a deadly agent. Each one held the ability to destroy countless terminal paths of a microchip. There must be enough dust in this room to destroy the world's supply of microchips he thought to himself. As if on cue, he sneezed. As he regained his composure, a man wearing a tailored gray three-piece suit entered the room. The man's smile was larger than life. Paul had seen a picture of him in a magazine with the same profile. This was the president in charge of the Strategic

Defense Initiative Program Department of Wescon Industries; a former somber General of the Air Force turned high-tech marketing executive. Paul stood and discovered that his five foot ten inch height was dwarfed by the six foot four figure. He engulfed Paul's hand in a firm embrace.

"James Moorehouse, welcome aboard." His voice was deafening. Having extended his brief diplomatic manners, the General turned and headed for his chair.

He methodically pulled out a rosewood pipe from his left inside pocket and placed it on the desk. One final check to verify that all was in its place, and then he sat down. Paul re-seated himself too as he examined the pipe lying next to a clean crystal ashtray. The slight aroma of Cavendish tobacco smoke swept across the room. General Moorehouse never went anywhere without this charred rimmed pipe. It was more than just an artifact of nostalgia; it had once indirectly saved his life. That is to say, back in Korea, he once left the pipe at the officers club. Upon remembering where he forgot the rose wood pipe, he left own tent and went back to the club to fetch it. He found the pipe all right, but upon returning to his private quarters, he found them to be gone; blown off the face of the earth by one of his own men's bombs. If they could have hit the enemy with the pinpoint accuracy that they unwittingly used on his hammock, the war would have lasted longer. However, precisely due to their inaccuracy, lack of results, and to others who performed just like them, both sides could not economically endure further escalation of hostilities. Therefore, the pipe saved his life, and the war ended early.

"I think you'll like working for our company," Moorehouse stated matter-of-factly. He sat behind the desk in the large shiny black chair. He moved around in the chair trying to get comfortable, but appeared to give up. He settled back in the unfamiliar chair. "Our department may be new, but most of the people employed here are already familiar with one another." Looking at nothing in particular he chuckled to himself. "I guess you scientific people are all like that. Not to be disrespectful," he quickly added. "I think it's good to know one's rivals or compatriots. But how you keep them strait when you bounce from project to project is beyond me." Paul viewed the General as a pompous ass, but considering the salary they were willing to pay him, this absolutely resounding first impression could be. Moorehouse began to feel a little uneasy with Paul staring at him. "I see you're a man of few words," he continued.

"We scientific type are," Paul callously replied.

"Good shot. I guess I had it coming." He smiled even wider and brushed back in place what little hair he possessed; pasted over the crown of his head a few sparse blonde strands tried to cover an area too vast; a real border patrol dilemma. Paul fought the urge to laugh. Why bother he thought, but then considered, he himself might be trying the same technique if his own follicle fallout rate didn't diminish.

"My people say your one of the best computer analysts in the country." Paul remained silent. "I heard you even worked on the National Air Space system. Air traffic control if I'm right." Paul remembered working for the FAA in the early 1970's. This man no doubt knew Paul's entire life history. If it was praise he was giving, Paul didn't need it. If it was historical leverage that would get him the job, then by all means, let the man ramble on. Moorehouse continued on portraying Paul's confidential consultant work on SAGE air defense system. Had anyone else mentioned his work on the later prototype system, Paul would have dropped dead in his tracks, but being a General with obvious ultra-clearance, nothing he might say would amaze Paul. Yet, still, he began to feel uncomfortable. Military references displeased him. They tended to make him feel guilty and taint his current ideology. At least he knew why this company had selected him. He thought about that a lot lately. A corporation out of the blue calls him, sends him letters, and wants to hire him immediately. He knew of them, but had not solicited. Somehow they found out what happened to his empire and were practically soliciting him the very next day. Still, he wavered for over a month. He knew how heavy Wescon Industries was involved with military contracts, and the prospects were unsettling. Finally, curiosity and finances got the better of him.

"Now the reason we hired you is not exactly to join the team, but to beat the team at every turn." Moorehouse paused, reached down and touched the pipe with his forefinger. He could see the glazed eyes that he had seen on the faces of so many other scientists that worked under him. Personally, he would take a foot soldier any day. They may not have an IQ of 150, but at least they paid attention and did what they were told. These guys on the other hand, had to be hand fed and kept in a constantly cleaned and sanitary environment. Otherwise they just fell to pieces. And orders: they had a mind of their own. A bunch of god damned Prima Donnas. Paul looked at the pipe. The General's grip around it was firm, his knuckles turned white.

"You see, we want you to look for faults in the programs our people devise as well as a couple of 'What if' programs we come up with. Now you won't be alone on this project, but then again, you won't be able to collaborate either. The way we see it, maximum saturation from different trajectories always yields the best results."

He smiled in triumph. A picture of him shaking hands with the President of the United

States of America lay on his desk. He examined the reflection his face cast off the glass casing. He gave a reassuring smile back at the picture.

"Sounds like it's going to be a time consuming task," Paul said.

"Oh, time is one thing we never have enough of. Hell, congress has us strapped with budget cuts for at least two years, and the laser hardware may even take longer. But the programming of COLD, Controlled Orbital and Laser Defense, has to begin at once."

"I understand," he said trying to suppress his disappointment. He didn't understand at all. He was hoping to work on the GATS program, not SDI. The GATS program he had read about in Scientific American. The GATS, Global Aircraft Traffic

Control Satellite system, was designed to give air traffic control towers a three dimensional view of incoming aircraft. Using land and space based radar-receiving systems; beacon signals from aircraft would be fed into redundant computer systems.

Information on velocity and altitude would then be used to form a three-dimensional picture in the control tower as well as relayed back to the aircraft along with any collision warnings or collision avoidance instructions. It could be a life saving system, and he wanted to be part of it. It was the first thought that came to mind when Wescon

Industries contacted him, but he guessed his background helped do him in. So he was stuck working on defense. Just as well he thought. The three dimensional guidance system used to aid aircraft, could just as easily be used to pinpoint or direct ballistic missiles. And what kind of a project was it anyway? In two short sentences he had been told there never was enough time and to hurry and get started immediately.

He felt being molded more and more into someone else's tool; a feeling he hadn't had in years, and he didn't like it.

"Now of course well give you a private office here and access to data related to your work. We won't make many demands on when you work; that's up to you. If you feel like working all weekend plus late at night, that's fine too. The facilities are always open. Just as long as you work, and work alone." He sighed and continued. "I can't emphasize that enough. We know that your human and that some of the people working here are friends of yours; that's Ok. You can visit, get together, what ever, but never discuss anything related to your job." Moorehouse looked very stem. He pointed his index finger at Paul. Paul wondered how much more of this schoolboy routine he could take. "That's the one cardinal sin. Things are different here than the rest of Silicon Valley." He looked at Paul as if expecting a reply of 'YES SIR.' The funny thing was, he had some kind of hold over civilians too. Paul felt compelled to answer. It was hard to ignore the man.

"That's fine." Just got on with the speech, Paul thought. Satisfied, Moorehouse widened he false smile once again.

"Now that we got that out of the way, glad to have you aboard." They got up to shake hands. The General's grip was rock solid. The pressure was firm, like a last reminder to let him know who was in charge. Moorehouse's voice took on a "best friend" type quality.

"Come back tomorrow and you'll be shown your office." He was then ushered towards the door. "Oh, one more thing," the General sounded almost apologetic.

"From time to time you might see someone check up on your work. However, if you should feel watched outside the company

Facilities, report it to us pronto. Those damned Russians and a couple of other unstable nations, will try anything to see what's going on in here." His poker face smile reappeared and in a perfunctory tone said,

"Good Day." He firmly ushered Paul out of the office and snapped his door shut.

Paul left the office more uncertain about things than when he went in. Cloak and dagger stuff was for the CIA; not for him. And that smile, that smile made his skin itch. But after losing almost everything, he needed the money; another usable pawn of capitalism. That's it, he thought to himself. He would work for a company over-funded by the government. No fickle consumers to dictate the company's future. No foreseeable layoffs, and most of all, a chance for advancement. He had had his chance at fortune and fame. Now he would just kick back in neutral, work a tedious and mundane analyzing job, and try to keep one pace ahead of the mounting bills. His neck and shoulder blades abruptly began to spasm. He couldn't lie to himself. If he could build a company once, he could do it again. He needed to reflect on the recent events. Accustomed to clear-cut goals, he wondered what would happen next. What would he tell his wife? His wife... Her soft voice and gentle hands messaging of his shoulders was suddenly all he cared to think about.

CHAPTER 4

Along the way home after the meeting, Paul drove past countless numbers of landscaping trucks and suspicious looking dark tanned men wearing worn out blue jeans. The men used hand held gas powered blowers to push grass trimmings away from the well-manicured lawns. His neighbors never worked on their own yards. In this part ofCalifornia, people worked hard at the office during the week and then left town on the weekends. Monterey and the coastline were less than an hour away due west. Lake Tahoe, Yosemite National Park, and Nevada gambling casinos were less than four hours due east. Northern California was truly paradise, in his opinion.

It was nearly noon and he thought he might be able to make it home in time for lunch. They had had roast beef the previous night, and this would be his last chance to get a roast beef sandwich before his sons devoured what was left of it. He didn't know which one was worse: his oldest son Henry, the football nut, or his other son Philip, who ran cross country all day long and ate all night. One more son would have left the cupboards bare and him malnourished. Oh well he thought, one more year until Henry graduated, three more years until Philip graduated, and then all that rightfully belonged to him could be reclaimed. It was a happy thought, but a somber one as well. He wouldn't miss the notes sent home from the local high school, but he would definitely miss the family weekend outings.

Reaching up on the visor, he pushed a button on a small plastic case and the garage door quietly opened. He gave a quick street appraisal of his four thousand square foot castle then drove the car inside the garage. The outside of the house needed a fresh coat of paint. It would have to wait a few paychecks. The garage door shut behind him before he got his own car door open. He crept into the house as silently as possible. He Up-toed past the kitchen and up the stairs to surprise his wife Helen.

"Mom, Dad's home," cried a voice from behind him. He cringed from the noise and shook his head in frustration. He had been betrayed by a figure searching through the pantry. No less in pursuit of the proverbial jar of peanut butter. Only one gargoyle shrilled with that distinctive tone of voice and used peanut butter to hold bread against the sides of roast beef; it had to be Philip. How that kid could run with a stomach full of sticky stuff was a mystery to him.

"It's all set. I got the job," he said as he entered her bedroom; he would never call it his. The only masculine thing in the room was a wilted palm tree in the corner next to his side of the bed. The rest of the room was filled with dainty peach colored ornaments. His wife tolerated the ratty looking plant only in respite. She was just waiting really. It was simply a matter of time before the browned palm leafs died and fell off.

"That's nice, we could use the money," she said in a warm tone of voice. She was busy folding laundry and barely heard what he said. She didn't even look up at him, her concentration was immense, and so was her dedication. To her, the more time elapsed, the more the clothes became wrinkled, and that was one of her biggest pet peeves. Helen was a blonde, blue eyed, woman who was aging beautifully, but looking at her lately left him depressed. He heard that many people divorced after their children left home; he wondered if it would happen to them. He couldn't think like that he thought. He just got a job. He was supposed to be happy.

"I'm almost finished. I won't be home for dinner, Francine and I are going out," she added hastily. She was wearing her new black and yellow striped jogging outfit. Her, just over the shoulder length, hair was held in place by a matching yellow bandanna. It was Wednesday: spa-day with a few of her friends.

"Want some help?" He asked.

"No thanks. I'm in a hurry and you don't do it right."

"You're welcome." He replied. He turned and went back downstairs.

Coming into the kitchen was like a scene out of Hollywood. Dirty dishes, pans boiling on top of the stove, and two fiendish ghouls stuffing their faces with whatever lay in arms reach. They were truly gruesome cannibals. The smell was absolutely nauseating.

"So you got the job with Wesson Industries?" He heard Philip's voice resonating through his glass of milk.

"It's Wescon Industries . . . Who's going to clean up this mess?" He demanded as he ignored Philip's question while he tried to spy the whereabouts of the roast. He hoped it wasn't already devoured.

"Philip's going to Dad. I've got to get going.' Henry, the traitor and frequent denunciator of his brother, gulped down the last of his glass of milk, tucked in his torn practice football shirt, and ran for the back door. The statement caught Philip off guard. With his mouth full of peanut butter, there was no chance to respond. He had been out maneuvered, but he knew he would get even. He would work on it after lunch. Henry gave one last triumphant smile as he slammed the door behind him.

"I think your macaroni's boiling over." Paul could smell the distinct aroma in the air. The foul smell refused to associate with the other lingering odors, and was a frequent aroma that habitually permeated the house. What amazed him the most, however, was how his sons were not only oblivious to the smell of burning pasta, but to the taste as well.

He watched his son take one last bite out of his sandwich and slowly make his way to the stove. It was no big deal to him. Just a few more noodles stuck to the bottom of the pan. If he dug at the noodles with a wooden spoon, the noodles would break free, and hopefully, the Teflon coating would still stick to the pan.

"Where's the roast?" He casually asked as his son swept by him.

"Mom said to make some macaroni because there wasn't enough left," came the response in a slightly garbled dialect. Paul knew all too well that this translated into: We ate it!

"Well, I'll just have to find something else."

"You can have some if you want." His son held out the pot of macaroni so his father could see close-up. He absentmindedly looked into the pot of black congealed ooze. He realized what was in front of him, and almost got sick.

"No thanks, I'll pass." His son, undaunted, proceeded to mix the burned noodles that stuck to the bottom of the pot with the rest of the mess. Paul moved on to his stash of tuna fish that he had hid in the back of the refrigerator. It was his lucky day. The

Tupperware container he labeled as sauerkraut was still there. Inside the container, his tuna fish safely awaited.

"I thought there was sauerkraut in there," his son indignantly stated. Paul jumped and his head hit the edge of a cupboard door. It hurt for only a brief second, but that's not what bothered him. He couldn't figure out how his son could sit at a table with his head turned in the opposite direction, and still know what his father was doing.

"There usually is, but I made a mistake and put the tuna in it the other day." It was a sly response, one that had worked before.

"Oh," came the mumbled reply. Then on second thought Philip asked, "Who eats that stuff around here?"

"Your mother does, and so do I." He tried to sound irritated.

"Oh." Philip fell silent and glanced at his dish of burnt noodles. They just didn't look as good after finding out about the tuna fish, but he couldn't let the macaroni get cold and solidify. He shrugged his shoulders. He put some ketchup on the yellowish brown mound and began to eat again. The family, to be honest, never purchased sauerkraut, but that was Paul's secret.

Few words were spoken as both father and son ate their lunch. Philip finished his macaroni and remained at the table quietly looking around. He wanted to ask his father a couple of questions, but wasn't sure if he should. There was no sense in making his father mad at him if he could help it, but he just had to ask.

"Dad?" He waited for his dad to look at him, that way he knew for certain he had his father's attention. "I asked Mr. Brandon the science teacher about Wescon Industries." Paul wondered what was on his mind, but he hadn't expected this topic. The usual subjects were girls and cars. "He says Wescon Industries is the biggest contractor for the Star Wars program." Philip paused: he was still a little unsure of himself. Paul was accustomed to his son's line of questioning, but could only guess where he was being lead.

"It's called, The Strategic Defense Initiative Program." This was as far as he would comment. Anymore than this and his son, the future lawyer, would have him stuck in an hour-long debate.

"Yeah, right, anyway, I thought you used to be against the arms race?" His son had him. There was no escape. He placed his half eaten tuna fish sandwich down on his plate and meticulously wiped his hands with his paper napkin.

"I've given it a lot of thought, and the way I see it, as long as I work on defense programs as opposed to offense programs, I haven't compromised my moral convictions."

"How can you be sure that they won't change your defensive project into an offensive weapon?" His son quickly countered. It was obvious he had given it a lot of thought.

"That's what I'll decide on a case to case basis every time they give me a new assignment. There's no other way. But right now, we need the money, so I hope you can understand my position. I'm on a tightrope, but that's what life's about. Besides, officially, the arms race died when communism fell." He smiled to reassure his son. He was just too smart for his own age.

"I hear you dad." He didn't mean to hurt his dad by bringing up the money issue, he just wanted something to tell his friends the next time they gave him a bad time because his father worked for 'Industrial Warmongers." At least that's what his friends called it. He looked at the mess on the kitchen counter and felt even gloomier.

Paul could see it in his eyes.

"Now come on, as soon as I'm finished, I'll help you clean this up." He wondered what Henry held over Philip to get him to clean it up by himself in the first place. Never mind, he was afraid to ask. It only meant that they were up to something.

By the time Paul had rinsed off the dishes and set them in the drying rack, the house had been vacated. It was a peculiar sound that first brought the emptiness to his attention. The heavy thumping of his son's footsteps were gone. Nor could he hear the constant hustle and bustle of his wife. Helen left without saying a word. Only the occasional snaps and pops created by the settling of the house broke the silence. For the first time in three weeks, he was alone. Thoughts of unfinished projects raced through his mind, but where to start was the key question.

Walking into the living room he spied his latest issue of Playboy. The wrapper had been torn off, and the pages looked like they had been pressed between the couch seat cushions. This would probably be his last chance to see it before one of the boys permanently absconded with it, so he decided the first chore on his list would be a quick browse through his magazine. Thumbing through the crumpled pages, he folded it back in order. A pressed flat piece of popcorn fell out and on to his lap. Several times he had mentioned to the boys to get their own subscription noting each time that he had illegally obtained his first subscription at the age of twelve, but each time his reasoning was quickly lost. After all, they would explain: why should they get their own, when they could read his for free. It was true, they could read it, he only wished he could see it once and awhile. Sitting down in his favorite easy chair (the one he got for Christmas last year), he rocked back and forth in slow motion as he casually turned the pages. One of the best days this year he thought to himself. In the back of his mind he knew his life would soon get a lot more complicated. He closed his eyes to try and dismiss his feelings. Soon, he fell asleep, but he wouldn't be able to rest for too long.

CHAPTER 5

Timothy Winters furtively glanced up and down the shadowed tree-lined street. No obvious vehicles snared his attention. The street appeared deserted. "Rotten bastards" he thought. They could dam well blend in with the trees if they desired, and he would never know. Paranoia crept to the edges of his consciousness; it would grow stronger, until it overwhelmed him if he let it, and right up to the point where total rational thought deserted him. He reached in his pocket and pulled out a dingy gray handkerchief, his constant companion as of lately, to wipe at the fluid accumulating under his nose. Cocaine, it is a seductive mistress. So seductive, that many succumb to her wiles with the very first usage. Tim Winters became ensnared just so. One time use; forever addicted. He put the handkerchief back in his pocket and brushed his hand against a small plastic cylindrical container. Normally, he wouldn't carry it on his person, but lately, he needed more frequent hits just to hold at bay his inevitable crash. The tactile reassurance of the coke calmed him somewhat. He walked towards the front door of an upper-middle class house. A shinny brass lion head doorknocker was level with his chest. How pretentious he thought. He was hoping to find the man a little more down and out. He glanced at his watch. Ten minutes, that's all the time it would take to give him all the info, then get out. Tim didn't remember him being overly social in nature, so he was just his type. Tim opted for the doorbell and waited impatiently for him to answer the door. His nose needed wiping again. A large droplet crashed on the front of his shirt.

"Dam it," he muttered and wiped at the damp spot. He knew he should see a

Doctor, but at a gut level he knew what a Doctor would say. "You've fried your septum, are you going for your brains too?"

"It's all right," she insidiously whispered from the pocket. "Soon . . .soon."

Timothy patted his pocket one last time.

Paul woke with a start to the ringing of the doorbell. A surge of adrenaline swept over his body and he wanted to wring the offender's neck. A sign by the front door read "No Solicitors", but there was a catch: most solicitors couldn't read anything but the label on the product they peddled, or thought their product was too good to let a mere sign stand in the way of the opportunity of a lifetime.

"If it's that religious group again," Paul muttered as he approached the door. He hoped the tone of his voice would scare them off. He opened the door and stared at someone who looked vaguely familiar. A thinly built man with short red hair wearing a rumpled gray suit stuck out his hand.

"Paul Crellin, Do you remember me?" Paul stared at the sick looking figure for a split second, and then recognized him. The two of them had met briefly on a few previous occasions. Besides being an employee of Wescon Industries, he was someone respected throughout the computer industry. Like Paul, Timothy Winters had had his hand in almost every major developmental project that passed the foremost drawing boards over the last ten to fifteen years. This, however, was the first time they were employed by the same company.

"May I come in?"

"Of course." What a shock to see him here! Even worse: to see him in his present condition. The Tim Paul remembered was young and vibrant. The man in front of him looked old and ill.

"Do you have a cold?" Paul asked. Tim's voice sounded deeper than he remembered and he could hear an occasional sniffle, Tim entered the house.

"Just a slight allergic reaction, nothing contagious." Tim made his way over to a chair and sat down with an overcoat folded across his lap. He pulled some Kleenex out of his pocket and used it on his dripping nose. He sounded like a foghorn as he blew into the Kleenex tissue. By the time Tim had cleared his sinuses, Paul had set the Playboy aside and sat down again with his arms folded. He narrowed his eyes and wondered why he had let in someone so obviously ill. He was probably in his most contagious stage what ever it was.

"Oh, don't worry " Tim said as he read the concern in Paul's eyes. "I've had this problem for over a month now and it doesn't seem to be getting better. But I didn't come here to talk about me, so here it is." Tim fell silent as he fumbled with the lock on his briefcase. What he was about to do bothered him personally, but orders were orders, no matter who gave them. "I thought you might want to have a look at this," he began as he pulled out a black folder. "I figured this would be the best way to speed things up."

"What is it?" Paul asked.

"Its a outline on Wescon's computer system. I've included access codes and ways to go around the security system. This is strictly confidential." Tim handed him a thick leaflet of computer-tabbed paper.

"But why give it to me?"

"Because you're the only one I can count on."

"Count on what. What's this all about?" Tim ignored his question as he blew his nose again.

"This gives you home terminal access to the computers at Wescon. It's fool proof. I devised it myself, and your the only other person who knows about its existence." Why was he showing him this Paul wondered He knew it could lead to Tim losing his job. What kind of risk was he taking to put so much trust in him? Just knowing something like this could put Paul at risk too. It was practically illegal in smaller companies, and with a defense contractor this big and well known, it was paramount to treason. He knew of others that disregarded rules of this nature claiming that they were the best in their field, so what harm could come to them? Yet, military secrets had previously been acquired by tapping into home terminals and he had known a few that were fired or worse for using home terminals, but such occurrences were rare. It was either because they were too sloppy to hide their entries, or the security watchdogs in question were highly skilled: although, most proficient security guards were quickly elevated to higher paying positions. It ultimately came down to a question of who could manipulate the computer network best.

Paul began to thumb through the pages. He scanned rapidly at the print, but he could only catch key words. He was just too nervous to concentrate under pressure. It had been that way all his life. He had always been a B+ student and it was largely due to his fear of exams. He might even have been over looked as a gifted student had it not been for his endless pursuit of answers. He questioned his professors whenever their office hours permitted. Only when he felt he knew the subject as well as they did, did he leave the haggard quarry alone. When it came time to be tested on the subject, he became sick to his stomach, and then his mind went blank. After the test scores were posted, next to his name was a high B grade. Just another fact of life; nothing he could do about it. Fortunately it wasn't his test scores that impressed the professors. It was his impressive ability to produce intricate programs, while still only a freshmen, that some graduate students couldn't even master.

"This is very interesting," Paul said as he finally grasped the meaning of a couple of paragraphs. The contents concerned security infiltration and prevention methods commonly used by Wescon.

"But why the home terminal?"

"Because time is of essence. I may be leaving the company soon and I can't think of anyone better to take my place. This is just between you and me . . . you understand. I can't promote you myself and you might not accept the job at this point in time anyway, so that's why I'm giving you this information. Once you get involved, you won't be able to say no. There is a lot at stake here. Not for the company, or me, but for the entire nation. I'm putting my trust in you now, so maybe you'll be willing to trust me later on."

"This is all too sudden," Paul said. He tried to hand back the papers. Tim waved them away with a hand gesture and continued.

"I know you're not a big fan of defense contracts, but we have three SDI satellites already built. Another two will be ready soon. All that's left will be the final programming, and in course, the installation of the laser system, which is already ten years behind schedule." Tim rolled his eyes and sighed. "In reality, a break through could produce a functional laser system in less than two years." It's not my intention to win you over to the strategic arm's race or what's left of it, I would just feel better knowing you're informed enough to help out in case something should go wrong." Paul suspected something had already gone wrong. Why else was Tim here? Tim was shaking and he seemed to turn pale. He fell silent. Both men were lost in thought.

"Well' if you don't have any questions for the moment, I'll see myself to the door." Paul was busy looking through the papers and mumbled good-bye as Tim headed for the door. "Oh, just one more thing before I go." Paul looked up at him. "I won't bring this subject up again. As far as the company is concerned, this meeting never took place. I hope you'll have enough trust in me to agree on this point." Tim knew he didn't have enough time to convert anyone else; he had to put Paul in his confidence. He heard Paul was as straight as a boy scout. He felt reassured that he could use Paul's patriotism against him at some point in the future. He might even be able to persuade Paul to spearhead the SDI's programs progress.

Tim smiled in the rearview mirror as he drove away. He felt the meeting had gone extremely well. He drove away feeling optimistically good about the encounter.

As soon as Tim left the house, Paul returned to his study. He had to know what this was all about and the sooner the better. On closer examination of the papers, he surmised that to review the data Tim gave him would be very time consuming. The basic program making the killer satellites operational had already been developed. The crude system could theoretically knock down a nuclear-armed missile with at least seventy-five percent accuracy. The goal was a hundred percent. The defense system itself worked on a three-tier arrangement: The missile launched, it broke the outer atmosphere, and then it descended. His task would be to analyze the program, see if the security system could be broken into by the Russians, Chinese, or whom ever, and in essence, be altered in a manor that would be advantageous to their side. He realized immediately what it meant. Tim wanted him to start out in security infiltration and prevention, and then as time wore on, plunge him deep within the fifteen million lines of computer input! And under whose authority was Tim asking him to work? Under

Tim's own nefarious authority? Under covert authority by the company? Was this part of a sting operation? Or possibly, there was yet another reason for this back door entry into the SDI project? Maybe he was just being too skeptical. One thing was for certain, everyone seemed to be directing him right down the hot bed path that lead to SDI programming. He could only think: With a little blood on his hands, he was already an accomplice. Admittedly though, he did feel a slight sense of exhilaration in just considering to work on such a grand scale. What would they ask him to work on next? Or better yet, how soon before he'd find himself heading up the offensive weapons program department?

CHAPTER 6

"Dad, I think you should take a look outside," Henry said as he opened the door to Paul's study. At the moment Paul was busy going over bills and other household matters.

"What's going on?" Instinctively he stood up. His son's call sounded urgent.

"There's a blue van parked down at the end of the street. I think they're spying."

A sudden chill snaked down Paul's back.

"What makes you think so?"

"When I rode by on my skate board they had the door open and I could see all of this equipment like a crime TV show. And they had this wire going underground."

They're tapping phone cables Paul thought. Illegal? Yes, but not surprising. Thank

God he wasn't on line and connected to Wescon's mainframe computer, or they would have caught him red handed. Already he had been working on the security project for well over three months, and his assignment was winding down to completion. By modifying the bulk portion of the program at home, he was able to relax and take life a little easier, and easier it was. He resigned himself to this new attitude soon aiter loosing his company. Recently, he hung around the office so little he got the nickname "Mr. Mystery". Along with his newfound attitude came the acceptance for this trite attempt at labeling him.

Now he wondered if his complacency towards rules might cost him his job. Had he been clever enough? He couldn't say for certain. He hadn't worked from his home terminal on company business in over two days. For the time being, the connection would remain severed. He couldn't afford to get caught. He had to find out what they were up to.

"Stay here," he said to his sons as he headed out the door. "Because my job's classified they're probably just doing a mandatory checkup."

The van parked at the entrance of the cul-de-sac stuck out like a beached Blue

Whale: a subtle telltale of the FBI? Walking across the street Paul noted the wires leading from the van to the cable box junction. The junction box was hidden from view by a shrub that seemed to grow in the summer and die in the winter. Today the green branches were pulled back with bright black cables exposed for all to see.

They might have as well painted a sign to announce their arrival.

"Oh shit," said Special Agent Curtis. He was sitting in the driver seat of the van.

"Here comes our mark." Agent Curtis forgot that they were supposed to be noticed, so he sat there looking bored, hoping the man under surveillance wouldn't notice them.

"Excuse me," Paul said as he tapped on the driver's window. A frowning face looked through the glass partition at him. Agent Curbs continued to chew on his well-worn piece of gum. Paul didn't like being ignored.

"Are you guys working on the phone cables, or is this supposed to be a secret?"

He shouted into the opaque window. A circle of fog formed on the glass. The window finally slid down.

"I don't like sarcasm," Agent Curtis replied. He proceeded to remove the gum from his mouth. The gum stuck to his fingers. He moved his fingers back and forth until the gum dropped and fell to the ground next to where Paul was standing. Paul looked up from where the gum landed and into Agent Curtis's unshaven face and into his eyes. Behind those hazel orbs, there seemed to be flashing neon "Vacancy" signs. "I'm just doing my job," Agent Curtis continued. Another fresh piece of gum slid into the leit side corner of his mouth and he proceeded to wear away at it.

"What's going on?" echoed somewhere inside the van. Paul tried to see inside, but a curtain draped behind the front seats blocked his view.

"Some guy is here bothering me." He could have said Dr. Crellin, for he recognized the subject at once. However, Curtis was playing it cautious. He didn't want Dr. Crellin to know that he knew who he was.

What an idiot, the man sitting in the back thought. An imbecile was schlepping around Two and a half million dollars worth of high-end equipment. Someone in the department was watching over this idiot. He peered through the curtain to look for himself. He ripped off his earphones immediately. Within seconds the side panel-door opened and a well-built black gentleman stepped out. Standing by the curb, Paul could see that the man, who rippled with muscles, towered over him. Paul felt a little uneasy.

He watched closely as the man smoothed out the wrinkles in his well-worn dark blue sports jacket. One final adjustment to stretch out the creases in his pants, then he stepped up to Paul.

"Special Agent Simson," a deep southern drawl informed Paul. "Federal Bureau of Investigation. Would y'all like to step inside for a chat?" Paul stared at the, six-foot three, figure and weighed his options. Unfortunately, his adversary out weighed him two to one; his options weighed less. Simson stepped aside and ushered Paul toward the open door. Simson smiled and nodded his head. His intimidation tactics worked so easily. It was funny he thought, the affect his frame had on people. A mild college graduate of Anthropology whose mere presence spread Neanderthalithic proportions of paranoia. That was how one of his former associates described him. That man was now dead. His violent death during a drug smuggling investigation in Miami gave Douglas Jonathon Simson the initiative to transfer to the west coast. It was never proven that the man that killed his partner was an undercover law enforcement officer; a CIA man bringing drugs into this country in order to exchange his goods for cash to send back to sympathetic forces abroad. To try and prove that would have meant his own death. Still, he couldn't sit there knowing what he knew, and do nothing, so he left. His cat and mouse games with foreign agents in silicon valley proved to be a healthier challenge. Besides, out here, it was easier to distinguish the good guys from the bad guys. Miami had too many shades of gray. A black, minority man, could go farther out west.

"Grab a chair." Already he was adjusting to the California lifestyle, and the short phrases he quipped, sounded more like a surfer than southern gentry. Paul stepped inside and was amazed by the high technology crammed into the tiny interior space.

"All this and room to stretch." Simson's relaxed manor of speech only helped put Paul more on guard. He felt the man was after his life. Paul knew the laidback speech was just a ploy to distract him.

"Simson eh? Isn't that Norwegian?" The big man looked surprised for a moment, and then burst out laughing as he settled back in his chair. He liked a man with a sense of humor, even though he know it would make his adversary, more cunning and potentially more dangerous.

"That's right. You might say I'm from southern Norway." He continued to chuckle. Paul laughed too. This special agent sitting in the seat opposite him no longer looked so ominous. He seemed to be the kind of man Paul would like to get to know better had the circumstances been different.

Paul turned his attention back to the van. From the outside the van appeared as if it had seen better days. It had rusted dents, chipped paint, and lopsided back fenders. The interior told another story. Four comfortable captain's chairs, each able to swivel three hundred and sixty degrees, bolted down to the brown-carpeted floor, gave easy access to all display panels. As for the equipment, electric circuitry ran the entire perimeter of the back half of the van. A real work of: state of the art technology. A faded dark brown curtain, Paul noticed earlier, hung on a flat-black metal rod crossing the cabin just behind the front seats. Apart from the small slot that Simson had previously peered out, the back end was essentially sealed off from outside eyes. Boy, he thought, what his sons would give to use this van on their dates. This was exactly what they talked about while sitting down at the dinner table. Although they never came right out and said they wanted a van for dating (they skirted this aspect), he knew what they meant, for he wanted a van of his own when he was in high school. It had two front seats, wall to wall carpeting in the back end, the perfect place to take a date. Funny how some things remained the same, even after some twenty years. Simson was proud of his requisition and gave Paul a minute to admire it. Time was one thing he had plenty of. He learned long ago that if you give someone enough time, they'd usually incriminate themselves.

"I had the roof raised myself." He reached over and turned on the ceiling lights.

Then he reached over and swung the side door shut. The interior darkened, but not as much as he expected. Paul recognized the faint aroma of a hot dog and glanced over at a trash bag stuffed full of garbage.

"To begin with Dr. Crellin, it never hurts to spread a little fear here and there."

"I thought they only did that in The Soviet Union or what's left of it." Simson merely smiled then gave a disgusted look at his temporarily assigned partner, Agent Curtis who did little else besides chew his gum. Agent Curtis turned around as he pulled the curtain shut. Curtis was six months away from retirement, and could give a shit what the Bureau did to him. With his seniority he could have been in charge of the surveillance van, but instead he preferred the lame duck approach to his career's uneventful conclusion. Never shown potential; never had to use his gun except on the range. He was the proud killer of dozens of paper clay targets. He rolled up his window and leaned back in his seat. He lightly listened in, as he thought about his cabin in eastern Oregon. Six more months and it was all the trout fishing he could handle. He was smart to play stupid.

He was almost home free. Maybe that was why he was feeling kind of jittery; he tried to ignore the feeling.

"Like I said, you're not in trouble. We just like to check everything out, and we may be even able to use your help."

"So what do you want from me?" The man's drawl made the pace of the conversation excruciatingly slow, which grated on Paul's nerves. It was exactly the affect Simson wanted to transpire.

"It's the old game. We call it 'SPICE'. They're the five most common motives for selling out to the other side. It stands for Sex, Pills, Ideology, Currency, and Ego.Someone's dealing in spice and letting secrets out of the disk drive." He had made up the last phrase by himself and was rather pleased by the way it had caught on with fellow agents.

"So where do I fit in?"

"Some of those secrets involved the GATS project." So that was it, Paul concluded. He had been asked to work on the GATS project when they were having some problems. He remembered that week well. All departments had been pooled to work on the GATS project to get it ready for inspection by a few key senators. He enjoyed the assignment and wished he could have been assigned permanently to GATS, but it didn't happen. The project was a simple application of existing technology with relatively few creative innovations required, where the SDI project necessitated as much creativity as possible. A job so monumental, that Paul was just a cog in the wheel, albeit he held a vital role.

"But I only worked on that project a week," he said. His statement went unnoticed.

"At the moment we're just trying to find out how many people are involved. We realize you haven't been employed there long, but do you have any ideas?" Paul shook his head no, although, immediately Timothy Winters came to mind. He hadn't spoken with him since the day Tim came over to his house. Whenever he saw Tim at Wescon.

Tim would either walk away quickly or become silent, which made the original encounter that much more eerie. The material Tim gave him was complex. He knew portions of it worked. But for the exact reason Tim gave him the material, he wasn't sure. Tim was likely headed for the funny farm. And that was one of the biggest reasons Paul never mentioned the incident to anyone. He hated to see someone as bright as Tim become a full time space cadet. And besides the mental health, Tim's physical health wasn't much better; chronically ill, runny nose, coughing bouts, and weight reduction. Paul wondered at times if cocaine, crack, crank, or, something worse was responsible for his physical condition. He knew cocaine could alter the mind, and he had seen friends rot out their nasal cavities with the junk. It seemed the most logical explanation, without really knowing more about Tim. And what about AIDs thing, he didn't even want to contemplate. He didn't wish that on anyone. He thought about discussing Tim's condition with him, but he didn't know how to tactfully approach such a personal matter. And was it any of his business anyway? Trying to show concern and pushing the matter further might have had the opposite intended effect. Anyway, his life was hectic enough without further complications. With Tim out of sight, so went his problems.

Paul's mind then began to wander off and contemplate his own problems; maybe not as great, but still bothersome. His own two athletic, sandy-blond hair sons had entered the world of heavy dating. Every time he turned around a different girl was lying on the living room couch, sitting in his own personal chair, or tying up the telephone line. The New York stock exchange trading floor would have been a quieter place to work at, than his own home. It was a wonder that he got anything done at all. He made his sons get their own phone thinking this would solve one of the problems, but he was dead wrong. If the girl called and couldn't get through on the boy's line, she'd call the house to ask why the other line was busy. How could he get any work done when he felt like a page operator? He only wished that he had had the good fortune that his sons were enjoying. Then again, he wondered how long it would be before one of them found their self in a delicate situation. The girls that worried him the most were the one's that constantly tried so hard when it was so obvious his sons could care less. Maybe he was just worried because of the similarities to his own past misfortunes. He wasn't ready for Grand fatherhood, and boys were rarely sane. At this hormonal age their lower brain controlled their thought process. "Perfume Stimulated Neural Transgression, PSNT", that's how one of his biology friends described the phenomena. It's difficult when a perfect stranger makes 90 percent of the decisions; one of his friends commented when talking about teenage male genitals. For that matter, the comment applied to males of all ages. Now all he could do was wait till their real brains came with age.

Simson sat quietly wondering what was going through the eccentric's mind. He envied the man's IQ, but hoped to hell he never became such a space cadet.

Paul turned to thoughts of his wife. Most of the time Helen either attended social events or stayed with her friends until five in the afternoon. The most productive period of time was when she was out of the house. On the days she stayed home, he could never get any of his work accomplished, let alone started. There was always one thing or another that required his undivided and immediate attention. Yet, when she attended her organizational meetings the house defended itself admirably against all crises. However, if it hadn't been for her errands, he might have been caught red-handed transmitting scrambled computer commands across the telephone cables. They might not be able to unscramble them, but the implication would be unquestionable. He sighed with relief and looked with renewed interest at the surveillance gear.

Paul felt the man's stare, he hated to be caught off guard. He realized he had been daydreaming again. He felt compelled to say something; anything to overt the manes staring eyes.

"Sorry I can't help you." He tried to keep his answer short as possible. He had heard long answers enhanced suspicion. He read this somewhere years ago. He tried to think where he had seen the article. Simson couldn't tell if he was hiding anything. He almost expected him to name Mr. Winters, but either he didn't personally know the man already under investigation or there was another reason. From Dr. Crellin's profile he had decided he was basically honest. He had some misfortune with his burgeoning company, but nothing to make him desperate. Not one single profile of SPICE fit him. Still, GATS secrets had surfaced in Florida, a well know gateway to Europe. So, just to keep him honest, the agency decided to instill a little fear. Aiter all, they reasoned, you can't retrieve national secrets after they've gone public. The CIA taught everyone this lesson. And after the CIA's spy problems they concluded it's easier to keep a man in line in the first place. That way you don't waste time patching up any breaches in national security. You can call it old KGB ideology, or a throwback to Gestapo tactics; it doesn't matter. The results justified everything.

"Now just between the two of us," Simson leaned closer and appeared more amiable. "I would play it safe and work strictly in the confines of Wescon Industries."

Paul tried to keep a straight face. Inside he wondered how much the man was going to tell him he knew. "We know you're one of the best in the business and can make those computers believe anything you tell them. I also doubt that most agents could ever catch you if you did manipulate them-at least not right away. But others have tried, and we always catch them. I hate to brag, but I'm especially good at all this equipment.

"So do us a favor or else we'll keep this van parked out here permanently."

"I've never thought of working anyplace else." Paul resented the threat and his tone of voice expressed it.

"Good, then we'll be seeing you at the office on a more regular schedule." So that was it, pure speculation due to his absenteeism at work. They had nothing concrete on him. His muscles relaxed. He felt chilled and realized his condition was caused by the van's air-conditioning system blowing against his heavy perspiration soaked clothes.

"As long as the office stay's warmer than this van, I'll be there." Simson detected the uplift in Paul's mood. He wondered what had caused the change? You're only the best until your caught, Simson heard himself recant in his mind as he admired the brains sitting next to him one last time.

The opening of the side panel door brought in a rush of fresh air and Paul felt the warmth return to his frozen limbs.

"Well, we know where to reach y'all," Simson stated then added ominously as the finishing touch, "should we feel the need." They both stepped out of the van.

"Right," Paul turned and walked leisurely across the street. Simson leaned on the van for a moment then hopped back inside. Paul never looked back. He kept his eyes fixed straight ahead on his family standing in the doorway. He wondered what he would tell them.

"What happened Dad?" his oldest son Henry shouted before Paul reached the driveway. Paul did not hear him. He was to busy concentrating on the sound of the van as it drove away down the street.

"Paul I want to know what happened?" questioned Helen's ever-authoritarian voice. Her worried eyes searched his very soul. He had to look away.

"Let's go inside first. I don't want any of the neighbors to hear this." He entered the house. The rest of the family followed him close behind. He headed straight for his favorite chair. The chair was unoccupied, and he was determined to get to it first.

"Well," he started out in a soft tone drawl similar to the agent he just met. "That's the Federal Bureau of Investigation. I guess I'm getting a little too well known." He tried to humor them, but it didn't work. Helen could see right through him and it was times like this that she especially hated his ill attempts at humor.

"What did they want?" she demanded. He looked at the tribe huddled around him. He was beginning to feel like some weird creature on public display. Their faces were stem and showed no signs of giving up the inquisition. He sighed, rolled his eyes, and then gave in as much as he dared.

"I'm not in trouble, so stop worrying. They are investigating someone else at the company and thought I might be able to help them. That's about all I can tell you." This appeared to have some effect, but he knew the question and answer period was far from over. He could play down the situation and his sons would quickly forget, but Helen was another story. She never tired; she always got what she wanted. Once focused, she could not be dissuaded, and her ability to interrogate was inescapably effective. Agent Simson could learn a thing or two from her. He settled himself more comfortably in his chair, trying to appear unconcerned, as he listened to the van drive down the street. He wondered how soon until they'd be back.

CHAPTER 7

Timothy Winters glanced around the deserted parking lot. It was just another misty night in South San Francisco. He checked his watch. It was almost midnight. From time to time the moon darted between the darkened outlines of buildings, shed a little illumination, then ducked back behind the clouds to recharge itself before its next inevitable foray. Streetlights surrounded by foggy halos gave him the only real constant source of illumination. He leaned next to the side entrance of a local grocery store. A few of the letters in the store's name were broken or missing. A couple of the large front windows were cracked, but it was obvious the owner didn't seem to mind. The store closed at ten and most of its lights were turned off. From his shadowy observation post he peered at the mostly deserted parking lot. At the far end a cluster of cars were parked by the local bar. They were small, banged up, economy cars. They were the second hand cars of an over-worked class of people trying to let off steam by having a beer or two before going home. He could use a drink too, but he decided it was better to stay out of public view until he completed his business. A gust of frosty wind ripped at his coat. The wind swirled around him sending small pieces of debris between his glasses and eyes. His eyes were temporarily forced shut. He wrapped the coat tighter around his body and shoved his hands into his pockets. His fingers rummaged through the remains of several candy wrappers. He rested his right hand against the package he carried. His eyes reopened with a sense of distrust for everything in his peripheral view.

The weather wasn't supposed to be so cold, but an ocean breeze worked its way over the top of Pacifica, swept past the Filipino capital of Daily City, and rolled down the entire peninsula. It's estimated that more Filipinos live here than in Manila, the capital of the Philippines. Only family bonds kept them huddled so close together in this cold and damp region of the peninsula. In Tim's opinion, anything north of Redwood City, approximately forty minutes south of San Francisco; bordered on the edge of Canada. A ten-degree thermo cline just north of Redwood City gave credibility to his theory. He predicted the temperature was now down in the low fifties. He considered the weather harsh for a native of Southern California.

At the other end of the parking lot a few empty oilcans noisily fell out of a trash bin and rolled aimlessly around the gas pumps. Earlier, he watched a longhaired teenage gas attendant collect them and throw them away as he lethargically went through the motions of closing down the station. The sporadic grating noises emitted by the teetering cans began to get on Tim's nerves. He checked his watch again: five minutes aiter midnight. The rats from the newly reformed KGB would soon arrive. He hoped the fog was miserable around Knob hill where their antenna-riddled embassy was strategically and advantageously located. The Russian intelligence group could intercept more juicy, and sensitive, pieces of gossip than they could ever handle from this prime location. He asked them how they could continue to operate when he had heard that the KGB had been dismantled. They never answered his question. He just figured the old KGB holdouts were merely determined to stop America's domination of the world. The fact that Japan really dominated the world, economically, didn't sway their intentions in the least. The foul weather would serve them right! Why did he have to meet them half way anyway? South San Francisco was a ghost town at night; a safe place to conduct transactions, but he had the information, so he felt he should have had the final say so on where to meet. The Russians had him and he knew it. He knew the layout of this neighborhood well, and that was the only reassurance he could summon from within. God, he hated these meetings! Tim looked at the cans with contempt as one rolled around on the ground until it fell off the curb and came to rest in the gutter.

He walked over and looked through the window of the vacated store. With an all night market one block away, and two major shopping centers close by, its no wonder this complex lost out. He stepped back from the window so as not to arouse unnecessary suspicion. He checked his watch again. This time he failed to make a mental note of the time. It was just the action, going through the motions that counted. He absentmindedly looked up at the broken letters that once spelled out the name of the store. Without the missing vowels, the sign made no sense at all. They are late. KGB were always on time. Something must have gone wrong. A man stepped out of the bar. One of the cars located near the bar turned on its headlights. Two quick flashes of light and then nothing. It wasn't his signal. He watched as the man from the bar stopped and looked over at the car. He wondered what the hell was going on. They must have thought the man was him, but that couldn't be right. The signal used was different. Each time they met, Tim felt insecure about the whole affair, but this time especially, he was emotionally on edge. His heart beat hard against his chest. He hated even the slightest change in details and now he wondered whether he should intercept the car and flag them over to him. They made a mistake. He popped two antacid tablets into his mouth. He chewed the gritty substance down until he could swallow. He glanced from side to side, and then proceeded to take a step in the direction of the car. Details or not, he wanted to get this over with. A sudden large racking cough shook his body and he had to stop. Large residual antacid granules rubbed and burned against the lining of his lungs and throat. He brought his hands up to his neck in a futile gesture. He heard the screeching of tires and the roar of an engine. A black BMW sped towards him. The car slowed down for a fraction of a second, then roared past him missing him by mere inches as it headed in the direction of the other car. He unavoidably inhaled a deep breath full of the car's exhaust. The windows were down and he got a brief glimpse of the driver. He thought he recognized him, but he had to be mistaken. There wasn't enough time to be sure. The BMW nearly sideswiped another car as it drove on. The suppressed sounds of automatic gunfire barely echoed off the buildings, but the cracking of glass and the pinging of metal quickly brought a multitude of rubbernecked gawkers out from the bar. Quickly, the midnight black BMW had exited the parking lot and now blended into the night; leaving the other car that had earlier signaled, riddled with bullet holes.

Patrons poured out of the bar. They were half drunk and half awe-struck by the carnal holocaust. Two bodies were slumped in the windowless car. By the time they had removed their gaze from the grizzly sight, Tim had vanished. He ran faster than a zebra chased by hungry lions. His lungs felt like they were going to burst. His legs, not accustomed to the heavy labor, felt on fire. He bounded over two fences and ran across several yards before reaching the car, which he earlier parked on a side street. The precautionary maneuver paid off. Traveling by foot he escaped unspotted.

On the way to his car the scene replayed in his mind. The face of the driver was calm and relaxed. As if he did this many times before. His mannerisms suggested he could have been just delivering fresh flowers, instead of deadly hot lead. It was all the same to him. So typical of the apathy the soviet old guard system propagated. His smile turned sadistic as he passed by. It was a strange look. As if purposefully trying to get Tim's attention focused on what was about to transpire. It was a warning Tim would never forget. As he sat in his car trying to catch his breath. He began to shiver. The same would happen to him if he ever out lived his usefulness. He started up the engine on and slowly drove away.

In the distance he heard several sirens converging on the scene of the hit. He watched as the flashing lights of a police car rushed by him. When his heart rate returned to normal, he checked his coat pocket. Another useless gesture; the packet of classified information was still there. He wondered whom he almost gave it to? Were they FBI? If so, then he had barely escaped one of their so-called sting operations. He should have worn a disguise. Then he remembered how he wore the coat wrapped around him keeping him virtually unrecognizable; he relaxed. The rendezvous was a complete disaster. There had to be a leak somewhere. He began to wonder if some of the information he was to deliver was part of a set up too? He hadn't bothered to review the information. He was already in so deep it didn't really matter. A quick glance at the information made him believe the info was routine in nature, but maybe he missed something. He was feeling run down when he copied the files. Maybe he should look at them again before trying to pass the info along. He reasoned, even a stool pigeon had his limits. Information worth dying for was out of his league. He laughed at the absurdity of what he just rationalized. He was diagnosed as having AIDS. His condition was going to get worse; it was only a matter of time. He determined how he contracted it, but this knowledge did little to relieve his burden. He still had to reconcile with the fact that he was eventually going to die. Only the former-Soviets and their experimental anti-Aids drugs promised him any chance at all. He wondered whether this incidence had already jeopardized his entire future. He decided to lay low for a few days while he tried to figure out what to do next.

It didn't take long for some of the bits and pieces to come together. The next morning on the front page of the Chronicle newspaper was the picture of the bullet-riddled car. The photo was black and white, but the bloodstains were still quite visible. No mention was made as to the occupants being FBI agents. That led him to suspect yet another organization was closing in on his illegal activities. At worst he feared that it was the clandestine CIA. Of course they would have to be operating illegally inside the US borders, which meant they would be as ruthless as the Russians. Well, maybe not that ruthless, he conceded. And people thought those tactics ended with Vietnam and the Nixon years. It would soon be time for another anti-Aids injection, he decided. He needed the Russians, for unlike America, they had not turned their back on him. He hated the way they treated people in the past, and he didn't know if democracy would get a fair chance in a country still politically thrown into chaos, but they had promised him something America could not, his life. Soon, he thought. They would help him eradicate the disease completely. Soon. In the meantime, the state of his health and his mental stability remained Questionable.

CHAPTER 8

Tim inserted a quarter into the pay phone. He called a number he had committed to memory, but never had to use. He was following a preset of instructions more than a year old. A system they had decided on when he had formally committed himself to the other side. With half of his mental faculties in a trance, Timothy Winters stabbed at the buttons of the pay phone with his index finger hoping the force applied with each blow would help jog his memory. It seemed to be working. He hoped to hell R did.

" Is this Mr. Smith? The total on your pizza came to eleven twenty five." He could hear someone breathing heavy on the other end. They didn't say anything else; they just stood on the line and waited.

"Ok, it better be hot, and don't skimp on the toppings," a deep harsh voice snapped back and hung up. His heart skipped a beat. They were calling him in permanently. Tomorrow at noon. They said to always delay things by one day plus half an hour. They would meet in front of a restaurant, and he was supposed to bring with him anything he thought he might need for the long trip out of the country. The word "hot" referred to the location. Camino Real passed through several cities and over forty miles, mostly north to south, along the peninsula. Some two dozen Chinese restaurants bordered the streets along the way. The one he wanted was a Szechwan, hole-in-the-wall not too far from the other ill-fated rendezvous site. Oh well, it was in their hands, what did he care. No matter what happened, if he wanted to live, he would have to do as his Russian friends demanded. His life depended on their decisions, their choices, and their charity.

He slept with her on several different occasions. Condoms never occurred to him. He just didn't think it would happen to him. Sure he knew she was a hooker, but at those prices, he took it for granted she was clean. Debra Long dealt from time to time with cocaine and that's how he met her. At first she just supplied him with dope, but that platinum blonde hair and curvaceous body was just too much to resist. She told him about her transactions with some foreign friends who told her they could help her. She told Tim she asked in his behalf if they could help him too. She said to him' "I have something to tell you. I have AIDS. You probably do to. But I have some friends who can help."

"Who?" He asked.

"Some friends. They have an experimental drug that can help."

"Where'd you meet them?"

"I meet anybody anywhere if the price is right," she bluntly answered.

A subsequent meeting was arranged and Tim found out just how foreign they were. The Russians said they were on the verge of curing AIDS and that they could help him, if only he cooperated. They gave him some pills and leit him alone for a couple of months. By then he was out of pills, but had already noticed a remarkable physical recovery. He was convinced they had the cure for him. He would never realize that what they had was a cure all right, but not one for AIDS. He was infected with a disease that mimicked, and would be diagnosed as the deadly AIDS related syndrome, but that's where the similarities ended. He would never know the truth. He would never know they set up this elaborate scheme sometime ago. The unfortunate truth though, was that without their help he would eventually die. The Russians could never be completely honest with him. Even with their medication he might eventually die. Their concocted virus never was completely stable, but it was the best they had. They needed the vital information only someone like Mr. Winters could give them. Being single, made him an easier target. So they tried it out. And just in case it didn't work, they had another scheme for Mr. Winter's possible replacement. Information was now more important than ever. If a country was going to rule, or keep from being ruled by others, that country had to be prepared, and implementing borrowed information was the cheapest way to remain prepared.

Tim discovered the Russian medicine was effective only temporary and he had to tell them on a daily basis. He also knew he might get caught passing on secrets to the former-soviets. These two reasons alone were enough to relieve him when he finally got the word to pack up. Maybe while working in Siberia or God knows where, they would come up with a more permanent solution to his infectious disease. Perhaps, if all went well, they might even give him a platinum blonde as his research assistant.

CHAPTER 9

"Hello," Paul said as he answered the phone. It was late and he was still working at the office. Two days elapsed since his encounter with the FBI. Since then, he conducted all work on his new project at Wescon's computer labs situated under ground, and in the middle of the defunct cow pastures. He tried to get in touch with Tim, but the attempt was futile. He didn't show up at work for the past three days and no one seemed to have any idea where he might be.

"Listen carefully," came a sharp reply. Paul recognized the voice's nasal quality. It had to be Timothy Winters speaking on the other end of the line. "I don't have much time." Paul had heard that phrase too many times before.

"Go ahead." He could only speculate on what Tim was up to. His voice sounded high pitched and frantic, but that was to be expected from someone who had probably gone over the edge one too many times.

" Meet me at Molly's bar at nine PM tonight. I'll explain it all there." The line suddenly went dead and he was left with a whirlwind of questions. He didn't want to go, but he couldn't turn his back on Tim either. Tim was in trouble, no doubt about it. He just wondered how much trouble and who with? A foreboding sense of curiosity would haunt him until the appointed hour.

Looking at his watch, he realized it was already eight thirty. He had only a half an hour to reach the designated spot. He knew the location. It was one of his old hunting grounds when he was single. He hadn't been there in years and wondered if it had changed much. Without delay, he locked the door to his office and left the Wescon complex. The evening air was chilly: about 68 degrees. The cool air helped clear his mind. Tim must be trying to avoid someone, he thought as he got in his car and drove towards the bar, but whom did he have to avoid? Was it someone from Wescon? It could have been the FBI, but Tim's voice reverberated with genuine life or death fear, and so far, the FBI was only using intimidation tactics. Then, all the rumors of KGB in Silicon Valley came to mind; but the KGB had been reformed. He tried to dismiss them. He hoped it was just a local Mafia problem. Gambling debt problems or something like that. At least the Mafia were business men and relatively civilized. A solution, whether or not mutually beneficial, could be reached with them. One, no doubt, you couldn't refuse.

He drove into the crowded parking lot. He recognized the blue colored van turning in and coming to a stop near the rear entrance of the structure. "Damn," he said. He hit his right hand against the dashboard. His phone line at work had been tapped. It was the only explanation. Obviously, he wasn't the only one that wanted to know what Tim had been up to. Whatever Tim was involved in, they probably believed he was involved with as well. He was sure of it now, a thought that didn't set too well with him.

Paul got out of his air-conditioned car. A blast of warm air caught him by surprise. The sun set over an hour ago, but the hot streak swept across the west coast yesterday still had not subsided. The weather was getting stranger all the time. He could never get over how in the space of a few miles the weather could fluctuate so much. He read somewhere the gap in the ozone layer over the South Pole was widening and some scientists believed we already entered era of the greenhouse effect. If this was so, he was sure California was going to become the next great dessert. To make things worse, the great quake was supposed to come at anytime. Facts like these lost their meaning in a land so rich with personal problems. With the seven pointer in 1989, San Francisco rebounded fast. Even the local Real Estate prices eventually crept upward again. It just didn't seem possible to loose all this in a cataclysmic event; no matter how many tremors he experienced, or regardless if man had a helping hand in the outcome; as happened with the burning of Oakland in 1991.

The strong smell of stale beer assaulted his nostrils. He checked the time, and then swept his gaze across the parking lot. Another five minutes until the appointment. The parking lot was full, and no one appeared to be waiting in any of the nearby cars. It was getting dark though, and soon would be impossible to detect anyone even remotely concealed in the shadows. He pondered over the idea of walking to the back of the building and saying hello to the guys in the van. But why ruin their fun? If they insisted with playing 'Spy versus Spy- Secret Agent Man', then that was their business. Besides, why create more animosity or suspicion?

He entered the bar slowly. He scrutinized every patron as if each and every one of them was spying on him. He was nervous. Hell, he was down right paranoid. The cool breeze from the air-conditioning system didn't help make the situation any more tolerable. The breeze was freezing the beads of perspiration on his forearms. If that wasn't bad enough, the music volume brought a slight sense of pain to his ears. Just the way his son's liked it, not him. The dance floor was small. Three odd couples of men danced with each other. Only a few stools at the bar were unoccupied. No sign of Tim.

At the bar he selected a seat next to a redhead. She had seductive brown eyes, full lips, and a body that he could still see when he closed his eyes. He could easily have fantasies about; maybe in another life or another place. He looked on his opposite side and was met by a smile of a guy wearing a peach colored short sleeve shirt. His lips were slightly parted. The tip of his tongue slightly protruded and moved from one side of his mouth to the other in a deliberately slow arched motion. The clear Polish on his fingernails reflected the surrounding light when he swirled his drink. He gave Paul a quick look over, and then batted his eyes. Being a piece of meat on display made Paul feel uncomfortable. He quickly turned back and gazed at the redhead. He would have surveyed every inch of her body, just like the man did his, but her face and eyes were so captivating he became immobilized.

"'Hello," said the seductive medusa. He nodded his head. His throat became dry. He absentmindedly rubbed his fingers across his wedding ring.

"Bartender, give me a beer on tap." It was all he could think of doing to stop staring at her. She knew he was mesmerized. She smiled and tossed her hair back. She was amused, but it was more than that, she would have felt self-conscious about her appearance if she hadn't commanded this response. She relished her sense of power.

" What type of beer do you want? " the bartender asked him. Paul looked over at the handles of the tap beer. There were four different types. Big gold plated handles with red, blue, and green colored labels.

" I don't care," he said. 'Just pick one.' The bartender leaned over and placed a mug under a faucet. He pulled on the handle marked extra stout ale. The 6.2% alcohol content tended to put patrons in a better mood, after which, he switched them back to weaker varieties. Being a bartender made him a good judge of character, and he could tell this guy was just too uptight.

"Here you go," he said and set the beer down on the counter.

"Thanks." Paul pulled out a five-dollar bill and set it down next to the beer. The bartender took it and quickly walked off. Paul wondered if he would ever see his change. It didn't take long to get the feel of the place and he was already feeling like he had been here a lifetime. In his youth, he spent a lot of time in places like this. His memories of drinking and hanging out with friends had been good ones.

The beer felt cold and sweet flowing down his parched throat. He hadn't had any for a long time. He never kept beer around the house for he thought it might spoil his work ethics. But now that he had a beer, he found himself looking forward to another. A couple of sips, and he was already feeling relaxed.

Thank God smoking wasn't the in thing to do anymore he thought as he remembered what the atmosphere of the bar used to be like. The billow of smoke had been replaced by flashing lights. The furniture was modern in design, but the bar itself had changed relatively little over the past fifteen years.

Paul watched as two bartenders exchanged words and pointed in his direction. Becoming curious, he snapped back from memory lane.

"Hey, is your name Paul? " The bartender working his section asked.

"Yes."

"Some guy told me to tell you he would give you a call on the pay phone at nine." He looked at Paul as if he were a little strange and began to walk away.

"Where's the pay phone? " He asked before the bartender got too far.

" In the men's room." He gave Paul a look of disbelief.

"Did he say who he was? " The Bartender shook his head and proceeded towards the other end of the bar. He acted as if Paul carded some contagious disease. He always found these situations a bit awkward. One of his drunks needed a refill and he didn't want him getting restless while waiting for another round. Besides, he had done his job. He was tired of setting up rendezvous for the gay community. But at fifty bucks a message, even he could walk a couple of steps and look the other way. What had happened to this place? It used to be a spot for couples. Lately, it had become a place for couples of the same sex.

Funny, but Paul had concluded the same thing as he watched a couple of women at near table. They were touching up their faces with make up. Their noses were unusually long and big for women. One of them had wrists and arm muscles as well defined as Paul's own. Two men holding hands soon joined the two of them in company. The men had nicely trimmed close-cropped hair, they were well dressed, and both looked very much in love as they caressed each other in front of the women. There had been a big change going on in the bay area and until now, he really hadn't bothered to notice. He didn't think badly of them. What they did was their own business. He only thought of one ramification. Single women must out number straight males in the bay area, eight to one. Things could only get better for his sons who had already shown themselves with traditional male role tendencies. His days as the telephone answering service for them would only get worse.

He glanced at his watch. It was two minutes till nine. Out of the comer of his eye. He caught the redhead staring at him. For a brief second he imagined her as Mata Hari. He was getting too keyed up he thought. He quickly dismissed the idea. He slid off the stool and felt the relief on the seat of his pants. Wicker chairs at a bar were definitely not the most comfortable things in the world. He took several steps towards the men's room before he regained full circulation in his legs. The redhead watched him leave. She picked up her Margarita and took a long savoring sip. With a slight toss of her hair she signaled to a tall muscular man to follow him. She hoped her friend Max, wouldn't have to be too violent. The thought excited her.

Paul entered the bathroom and found the pay phone next to a sink with water and soap splashed all about. Wet discarded paper towels littered the counter top, over filled the trash bin, and cluttered the surrounding floor. The blond hair man stood just outside the door. He held a cigarette lighter in his hand and patently waited. Fortunately, Paul was alone in the small cubicle room. Just enough room for one person to wash their hands while another talked on the phone. Handwriting shown on the walls even though the letters and numbers were covered over by a fresh coat of paint. "For a good time call . . ." most of them read. The room's lighting emanated from a single naked bulb on the ceiling. Chrome faucet handles helped reflect some of the light. Another door lead to the toilet fixtures. The overpowering smell of deodorizing tablets filled both rooms. Paul opened the adjoining door. He could see the shoes of someone in one of the two stalls. They were black dress dance shoes; polished, with clean soft leather soles, not the type that FBI agents used for legwork. They didn't look that comfortable for walking; just glitzy dancing shoes. Satisfied, he shut the door and waited. At precisely nine o'clock the phone rang. He picked up the receiver and said hello. Tim's voice shouted into his ear.

"Look inside the paper towel dispenser." The line went dead. Paul was still trying to comprehend what had transpired when the outer door swung open. A blurred figure grabbed the phone out of Paul's hand. A solid hand-chop came down sharp on the back of Paul's neck. Abruptly Paul felt his body being flung against the wall; swept aside like a piece of paper. The assailant held the phone next to his ear and heard the buzzing noise. He let the phone drop and used his free hand to press Paul's face hard against the wall. Paul's back went numb and the rest of his body seemed to crumble under its own weight. Fire shot out of a gas filled cigarette lighter only inches away from his face. Paul forgot everything else and focused on the blue and orange colored flame. Another inch closer, and he knew he'd be blinded.

"What did he say?" An agitated voice asked with a slight Slavic accent.

"He said he couldn't make it," Paul said in slurred syllables. His lips were pressed too firm against the cold rough surface of the wall to speak any clearer. The thought struck him that he might die right then and there for lying, but for some reason he said it. The fact that he was now still alive gave him a false sense of hope.

"Are you positive?" The door leading to the urinals opened. With one powerful sidekick the assailant slammed the door shut and sent the unfortunate bystander sprawling on the floor in the next room. At the same instant he yelled, "Wait a moment," and secured a stronger grip around Paul's throat and head. Paul thought his nose would break from just the pressure of his face being pressed so hard against the wall.

"Positive," he reaffirmed in a garbled tone. "I saw two FBI sitting outside. They must have scarred him off." The man released some of the pressure on Paul's head as he pondered the situation. Paul looked too puny and scared to hide anything. Paul caught a glimpse of the man's face and it was permanently etched in his mind. The light reflecting off of his contacts intensified his glaring eyes. In his right eye, the lens had shifted its position, possibly due to the sudden physical activity. An eclipse of a gray colored iris showed beneath the chocolate brown lens. He was definitely of Eastern Europe decent. Paul couldn't even begin to imagine how Tim had gotten involved with this lot.

"We will be watching you." He then shoved Paul down towards the floor. His face hit with such impact that his teeth cut through his bottom lip. He tasted the iron enriched liquid and saw blood on the floor. He brought his right hand up to his face to gauge the damage. The figure leaned over him. Oblivious of his temporarily incapacitated victim, he looked at himself in the mirror. He straightened his dress shirt and tie. He smiled at Paul, stepped across him, and walked out. Paul lay on the floor waiting for the pain to subside. He felt the door push against his back. He remembered the poor guy in the inner room. He rose to his feet to get out of the way. He felt a little unsteady, but he made it over to the sink. He left a trail of blood behind him. The other victim was living mad when he came though the doorway, but when he saw Paul, he only thought how lucky he had been to escape the brunt of the assault.

"Must have been on drugs," Paul suggested as he cupped his hands and brought the cold water to his swollen and cut lip. The upset man looked at him for a brief moment, and then decided to leave the place. He had had enough excitement for one night. He was going home. Paul reached for a paper towel and remembered what Tim said. His eyes riveted on the white metal container. He wondered if the contents had been worth the risk. The box was locked, but with a little force, he broke the compartment open. Inside he found a small envelope sitting neatly on the stack of paper towels. He quickly took the envelope and put it in his front pocket. When he removed his hand away from the dispenser, the lid swung down by the force of gravity and closed off angle. With a slight tug he pushed it into its normal locked position. He took a deep breath to clear his mind. He noticed the blood flow was now down to a trickle. Time to go he thought. Unfortunately, as he walked through the doorway, the two men from the FBI approached him.

"Would you like to step back inside?" the black man, Special Agent Simson, asked. His expression was stem until he noticed the condition of Paul's face. Then he looked almost as if he was disappointed.

"You're a bit late aren't you?" Paul stated as he rubbed his chin. The drying blood was beginning to itch. 'The KGB just frisked me and took blood samples, so I don't have a lot left to offer. Or at least that's who I think it was." From the looks of him, Simson didn't doubt his accusation.

"Can you describe them?" Agent Curtis asked nonchalantly while chewing on a piece of gum. He immediately thought that there must have been more than one attacker.

"Yeah, a tall blond guy with gray eyes wearing brown contact lenses."

"One man?" Agent Simson said surprised. "Sounds like someone we know. Did he tell you where you could reach him?"

"He said he'd find me."

Agent Simson sighed in disgust. "Mr. Crellin, sounds like were going to have to assign some men to watch you. That doesn't sound like the KGB, especially the newly reformed KGB. They are a lot more subtle now days, but if the people responsible are letting you look at them this closely, then you can be assured that your in a lot of danger."

"But I didn't do anything. Winters just asked me to meet him here and he didn't show up."

"Did he give you any clue as to where he might be staying?"

"No, but I'd sure like to find him." Paul tightened his fists to further emphasize his intentions. His actions were noted, but the two men were not swayed. Paul just looked too much like a wimp. Besides, they figured he was guilty until proven innocent: especially when playing with the heavies like the one Russian he described. That guy used to do milk runs. If he was indeed the one that came to mind, then he specialized in rubouts. He was one of the worst breeds of professionals. And worse yet, he had turned renegade. Aiter the failed Russian coup, he and some others left the KGB and were now working for God only knew.

Agent Simson's voice hushed. "Confidentially, Mr. Winters has been missing for days. It may be that he got himself into a situation he couldn't handle. You've seen the TV show 'Sixty Minutes' haven't you?" Paul nodded yes. "Then you know how it always ends. If he's involved with selling secret information, we'll only incarcerate him. The Russians however." He paused to instill more fear into his prey. "The Russians or whoever they call themselves are now, they'll kill him." Paul felt sick to his stomach as he tried to rationalize his actions. His condition was only made worse by the amount of his own blood he had ingested. He could only reason that if Tim could not trust these men, then he could not confide in them either. As bad as Tim had been made out to be, Paul was certain Tim had a conscience, and until he could prove otherwise, he would retain his trust in Tim. Hopefully, when he analyzed the contents of the envelope, he would gain some insight into this unfortunate predicament. Then again, maybe he might find only disappointment in Tim and himself being played for the biggest fool of all time.

CHAPTER 10

Prior to phoning Paul, Tim returned to his house after having spent the morning making last minute purchases and getting his finances in order. With few possessions and twenty thousand he previously borrowed from a home improvement loan, he was ready to leave the country. Twenty thousand may not seem like much, but he was assured that on the recently evolving Russian black market he could live like a Czar on such a paltry sum. The agents painted no rosy pictures about his new country. They flat out told him Rubles, the Russian monetary unit, were as worthless inside the former soviet block as they were outside. They had no reason to lie to him. After all, they didn't have to offer him paradise in exchange for national security secrets. They were offering him something better. They were offering him life. The greatest strategy they had ever come up with. Compared to this, SPICE was as worthless as their own propaganda-backed currency, and the best part was, that it might take the Americans another five to ten years before they figured out the scam. By then, the wall protecting United States secrets would resemble Swiss cheese, or at least the defunct wall enclosing Berlin. The Russians could focus all of their resources on keeping satellite countries together economically instead of militarily, which as of late, was costing them dearly.

Tim drove down his residential street and noticed two unfamiliar cars parked curbside not far from his tract Victorian home. In a neighborhood like this, a person knew everyone, or at least the cars they owned. After awhile you even recognized their friend's cars. The American made car did not fit any aforementioned description. He shifted down his 28OZ and drove past his house. He was glad he had opted to sleep in his car last night out in Pacifica. He kept a blanket in the back for those special occasions when he had a date that preferred making it under the moonlit night, and was able to keep warm. He shuddered at the thought of what his sexual prowess had caused him. His clothes were wrinkled and he had a kink in his neck, now two days running, but other than that, he slept quite deep. A reclining bucket seat and a little cocaine, that's all it took. What a life he thought. He felt himself spiraling down. Next he would be joining the bums in the mission district. They were pleasant, but what a life; homeless and bereft of the great American dream. He had to get out. America held little left for him. Escaping to Russia or one of its satellite states would be the cure to all his problems. There was a new and exciting country forming over there. He desperately wanted to believe so.

"That's him!" Agent Curtis looked up from his sports illustrated.

"That's him all right."

"Wonder where he's been?" Agent Simson already had a good idea. He had to have been with the Russians, if that's who they really were.

Tim saw the men in the car watch him pass by. They made no outward effort to follow him down the street so he felt he was safe. There was no way he could have seen the helicopter a thousand feet up quickly pick up his trail. He drove around a couple of blocks then circled back. It was already close to eleven and there was no way he was going to be on time to meet his contact, but that didn't really concern him. If he was leaving for good, then he wanted to stop at his house first. He planned on being quick, a picture of his mother, the only person that ever meant anything to him, and what was left of his stash of cocaine. He came back down the street half an hour later and the van was gone. With a sigh of relief, he parked on the street and walked up to his house. All appeared normal. He unlocked the door and stepped inside. There was no one waiting for him inside. It was just routine surveillance he surmised. They had done it on several occasions in the past. He was still in control, even if the Russians had gotten spooked. Upstairs in his bedroom he grabbed his mother's picture. It was taken before her hair turned gray. When she was proud of her college bound son. She said it would give him something to remember her by when he went back east to school. If she only knew how far he was going on this trip. He also took a handful of jewelry; some of it his, some of it passed down the family tree. Forget about clothing he thought. He would soon be attired in the latest Russian domestic attire, ill fitting, but less conforming in style than the old soviet days. He started to put the jewelry in his trench coat pocket, but was stopped by a package. He removed it and stuffed his pockets. With package in hand he went back down stairs. He went into the front room and set it on top of the coffee table. He reached under the adjacent couch and pulled out a silver rimmed mirror-tray. A gold razor blade and a small bag of cocaine set neatly at one end. He looked at it for a brief moment then gave in. Why not one last hit for the road? He set the tray on the table and expertly unraveled the plastic bag filled with white refined powder. He took out his key chain and selected a key. It looked like all the rest, but it split open when folded back on itself to form a small spoon. He dipped the spoon in the bag then brought it up to his nose. A few short sniffs and he felt a rush of energy flowing through him. "This is life," he enthusiastically said to himself. He leaned back on the couch. He looked at the package he'd found in the pocket again, but as if he had seen it for the very first time. He reached over, picked it up and opened it.

After examining the contents, an excellent copy of the originals, he began to write a note. The phone ringing stopped him. He picked up the contents along with the note and placed them back inside the package. The phone continued to ring.

"Hello?" He answered. The line went dead. He remembered his appointment with the Russians. Screw them he thought. There was time to finish his stash before he left town. The coke had altered his perception of time, space, the situation at hand, and why he even existed. The phone rang again.

"What do you want?" He sarcastically asked.

"Did you order pizza?" a gruff voice demanded. Tim became suddenly fearful.

"Yes," he answered hesitantly.

"We couldn't fine your address. Do you still want it?"

"Of course." His heart quickened. Of course he wanted to leave. How could he have forgotten? Without them he would die.

"You'll have to come and get it, our truck broke down."

"I'll be there soon as I can." His knee jerked, hit the silver the tray, and the tray sailed down to the carpet. White powder blew in all directions.

"We'll keep it hot." The line went dead.

"That's it," Agent Simson said. He was in the yellow Victorian house at the corner of the street. The one they had leased to keep surveillance on Timothy. They had suspected him for quite some time, but needed definite proof. And if they were real lucky, they could nab his contacts too. The phone tap had finally paid off. There was something big going on. He looked out the window and grinned with delight. Now he had him.

Tim wondered what he should do. Having examined the contents, something he never did in the past, he felt the moral implications. He just couldn't bring himself to give it to them. He decided to ask Paul for advice. He was the only one he could think of. He'd give him a copy and see what he could do with it. Molly's bar would be a good place to meet. They bumped into each other there in the past on one or two occasions, but he doubted if Paul remembered. Tim was not as well known as Paul in those days. He would give it to him. Then tell the Russians that after examining the contents, he found the information to be obsolete. It just might work. He took another hit, then picked up a small bag of belongings, and left the place a mess.

He drove straight over to Molly's to check out the setting in case he needed to alter his plans. He just entered the parking lot when he first felt he was being watched. The helicopter returned for fuel and a back up car was being used to keep an eye on him. Again he decided to change his plans.

After going into the men's room, he left the copies he made along with the half completed note hidden inside, he then had a few drinks, passed a note to the bartender, then left the bar. He never did finish the note. He forgot all about it. Down the road a couple of blocks he pulled over and called Paul from a pay phone. He wasn't home. He reinserted the quarter then made another call.

"Hello," the deep voice answered.

"I'm running late, I stopped at a bar."

"What bar?" the man was furious. The code had completely broken down. All he wanted to do was bring Tim in, and strangle him with his bare hands. Tim hesitated for a moment. He didn't really want to give the name, but he felt pressured. "Molly's Bar. I just left, but I think I had a little to much to drink." He could hear the man hissing on the other end of the line.

"Get here as fast as you can or we'll come and bring you here. You got that?"

"Yeah, I got that. But I'm still celebrating,"

"Get off the phone. You can have your party here." Tim hung up. That's what you think comrade. They were pissed with him, but that would all be forgotten when he gave them the package. Wait a minute, he thought. He was becoming confused again.

Back in his car he sniffed a little more coke. He sat there for a while just thinking about nothing in particular. Traffic rolled past him. The sun began to set. He remembered to call Paul. He went back to the pay phone. This time, he tried the office, his call connected. He asked Paul to meet him at Molly's. Tim got back in his car. He checked the time and finally realized that several hours had escaped him. The Russians could wait for him. They were the ones getting the bargain. This would be his last day for coke and fast cars. He was going to make the best of it. He would make another call to Paul. The Russians would most likely stake out Molly's waiting for his return, so he would have to move the party. He drove back to his house. He just hoped Paul could sort the whole mess out. In the mean time, he would have one hell of a night before he came crawling back to the Russians.

CHAPTER 11

Paul returned to his car, Paul sat back in the driver's seat and took a deep breath. His nose still hurt like hell. The FBI van slowly pulled up beside him. The two shadowy figures waited patiently inside the van. Why they did this he wasn't sure. He felt relieved in a way, for with them nearby, there was little chance of a repeat performance by that ex-KGB ninja commando. In fact, the near death experience today justified once and for all in his mind the necessity of such organizations as the CIA and FBI. The nefarious encounter not only gave him new insight, but also a few well placed facial bruises. He rationalized that while certain government agencies may have over stepped their authority from time to time like a guard dog escaped from its leash, they were still the best defense against the unscrupulous tactics of his assailants. So much, for the end of communism, the new world order of peace, and global prosperity. Some of the Russian old guard were still in business and only in business on and for their own behalf.

Paul inserted his key into the ignition. He recalled a movie where the very same act caused a car to explode into a hundred little pieces. The thought made him wince. The engine turned over in its typical high-pitched screech. It needed a tune up for quite some time. He relaxed a little; he was safe for the moment. He had to stop thinking like this. Paranoia was not the answer, he repeated to himself over and over. He kept asking himself why he allowed himself to get involved; his self wasn't sure of the answer. He didn't feel the need to be heroic. He didn't feel very committed to Tim. He didn't feel committed to anyone save his family. He couldn't explain it. Something deep within him made him want to covet the envelope he found inside the towel dispenser. Something deep within him also reminded him he could quickly get himself killed. Somewhere deep could be where they placed his casket.

He drove the car out of the parking lot. The van followed close behind him. He made a note of their distance. Better to be safe than sorry. He wondered how he would explain this to his wife? "By the way Helen, I stopped at a gay bar on the way home and got mugged by a muscle bound Slovenian in the men's room?"

There was also the nagging question as to how long this ordeal would last? He wasn't exactly the President who required twenty-four hour surveillance for the rest of his life. He couldn't stand that sort of treatment no matter how reassured he was by their presence. Shortly, the situation would be resolved for him. The van pulled off the road and Paul felt an anxiety attack coming on. He didn't want to give up his newly discovered security blanket just yet. Being guarded like the President, didn't look that bad after all. The rest of the way home he kept a rigid lookout for any signs of suspicious cars or their occupants. What he needed now was to purchase a gun: a small handgun that would fit in his breast pocket. He gave that idea up fast. He was no secret agent. He wasn't even sure he could lie convincingly, let alone kill a man in cold blood. It was all senseless, just like war. What would a secret agent tell his wife?

He pulled into his driveway. He turned off the headlights and shut off the engine. The car became silent except for an occasional pinging sound emitted by the cooling metal parts. The sounds of crickets drowned out all other noises. Paul rolled up his window and touched his pocket. The contents pressed against his leg. The souvenir reminded him briefly of the day's events. He exited the vehicle and surveyed the surrounding area. The street was barren. All cars were properly stored in their garages. In fact, he only saw one car on the main street before he entered the cul-de-sac. A dark colored BMW. It came to his attention because he always wanted to own one. He liked their style and liked their speed, but it was Helen who always said no. She didn't want to own one she said. Everyone else had one. So she drove a now Corvette that rumbled like a tank, and he drove a, 911, that he considered the poor man's Porsche.

He stood by the door and glanced around one final time. He inserted the key into the lock. The street was still quiet. No one jumped out of the bushes. One minute the sight of the van annoyed him, now he was upset with its' departure. Maybe his day of playing secret agent James Bond had come to an end. On a more sobering note, maybe his friend was nothing more than a thief, and he had helped obstruct justice. Deep down he didn't believe so, but it was something to consider. "Damn," he said in a low hushed voice.

He entered the darkened foyer as quietly as he could. In all the excitement, he forgot to call home. Because of this oversight, he would soon have to account to an authority more powerful than the KGB. He looked down at his watch. The dots glowed dimly in the dark. The sun already set long ago. Stumbling his way up the stairs, he tip toed up to his bedroom and peeked inside. Helen lay with her head down on a pillow. Her eyes were closed and she appeared to be fast asleep. Feeling a sense of relief, he descended back down the stairs into the shadowy abyss. It was time to examine the contents of the envelope in the privacy of his own study.

As he walked through the living room, he could still smell the faint aroma of buttered popcorn; clear evidence his sons recently occupied the room. He halfway expected to find one of his sons draped across the couch with one of their myriad of girlfriends. Tonight however, the room was empty. The couch pillows were in place. He walked on to his study situated at the opposite end of the living room. He opened the door and reached for the light switch on the inside wall. His hand made contact on the first pass. He heard the faint crackle of fluorescent tubes as they illuminated the study. He closed the door behind him. He pushed the main power button imbedded in the top of his mahogany desk. His desk lamp along with his computer system lit up. He did this like clock work. It didn't matter if he came in to use the equipment or just to read the paper. Having things ready, just in case, was the way he liked his life run. It was one of his characteristics that had distinguished him above others in his field, and yet, it was nothing more than the simple axiom he learned as a Boy Scout. "Be Prepared". He didn't feel prepared at all right at this moment.

He looked down at the stack of wrinkled papers and computer printouts that cluttered his desk. His son Philip had been using his computer again. The scene was beginning to be a common occurrence. He discussed the issue several times, but his son was as absent minded as his father. So the battle over everything in its place continued. He felt he was on the loosing side.

He gathered the pile in both hands and moved it to the floor several feet out of the way. Gazing at his clean desk top, he pulled out the yellow envelope from his pocket and set it down. He looked at it one more time in silence. He only hoped it had been worth the effort. Osmosis wasn't working, he took the envelope and held it up to the light. What a troublesome little package. The outlines of two small dark rectangular objects contrasted against the illuminated paper background. He had no idea what they represented, but for some inexplicable reason he knew he had to keep them to himself. He had to unravel the mystery. He tore one end of the envelope and carefully let the contents fall on the desk. Out dropped two IBM compatible disk tapes: the type of tape that held at least two hundred megabytes of information each. A folded piece of paper slid half way out, and then ridged itself against the sides of the envelope. He pulled it out the rest of the way with his fingers. Nothing seemed to go easy for him lately. The note was hand written in dark black ink. He unfolded the paper and read:

I hope this activates your interest. It's highly critical.

I'm sorry, but you have to stop...

The last few words were illegible. The writing was unmistakably Tim's. Either he ran out of time, or something interrupted him from finishing the letter. There wasn't a signature nor was it addressed. The entire situation was getting more frustrating with each passing event. Now, he would have to count solely on the contents of the two tapes to resolve this mess. He opened the plastic cover of one of the tapes and inserted it into his micro-tape player. He pressed several keys on the computer keyboard, and then pressed the play button on the tape deck. The computer screen immediately went black except for a small cursor-dot blinking on and off in the lower left-hand comer. In the meantime, the spindles of the cassette player spun the tape from one wheel to the other. Leaning back in his chair, he anxiously waited for the information to appear on the screen. Abruptly, the tape player halted. Some three minutes passed before the information formatted and filled the screen. Paul was aghast. He froze in his chair. He tried to compose himself. He rubbed his hands against his forehead and tried to swallow. His mouth was dry and the attempted action burned the back of his throat. It caused him to cough. He tried to swallow again. He finally succeeded. The sight had been too much of a shock. He couldn't visualize Tim as a spy. Yet, had he given these tapes to the Russians, he would have probably been ranked as the ultimate traitor. Displayed on the screen was project "Circuit Board". He knew about this sub-routine program from overhearing people, "In the know", and he also knew that this information was part of the Strategic Defense Initiative Program. He just couldn't believe it. A Trillion dollar project was on the verge of being sold out for probably less than a penny on the dollar. A quick role of the screen showed the tape's data was primarily related to security.

"'So that's why he came over that night." Paul took it out of the tape player and inserted the other tape. A short while later, the screen filled with more dark letters on a light gray background. It appeared to be a different segment of the same project. However, without a thorough analysis, he couldn't be certain. Too late in the night he thought. His body was already drained from the day's events. With some of the curiosity lifted, he placed the tapes back inside their containers. He carried them over to his bookshelf. He pulled down a book titled 'Life of the Aztecs,' he hollowed out the book in his youth. He put the tapes inside for safekeeping. Up on the shelf and beside a myriad of other books he placed his enigma. No one would ever find them. He gave one last sigh, and proceeded to turn his computer off.

As he turned off the rest of the lights and made his way up to his bedroom, his mind raced with questions. He imagined Tim stealing information to support a drug habit. This could have been the motive. Then again, druggies were desperate. A druggie wouldn't renege on a deal. He'd kill his mother to make a deal. And if he did have the sheer will power to renege, he'd be lucky if the former soviets didn't kill him. To risk death and to put himself in danger by both sides was suicide. Only a fool... No he thought. Someone still wavering over their moral convictions might do such a thing, but why? The tapes contained something that Tim was willing at one point to give the Russians, and then decided to thrust in his hands instead. He would have to search through the tapes for the answer. He knew it wouldn't be easy. If it had been a simple case of getting cold feet or regaining American patriotism, then Tim could have erased the tapes or given them to the proper authorities. He, Paul Crellin, had been specifically selected to receive the tapes. Therefore, the burden of solving the puzzle was left on his shoulders alone. It meant putting his own life in jeopardy, but he needed to know. There were few things in the world that had greater consequences than the misuse of Star War-SDI-technology. Used incorrectly, it gave a single man ultimate military and political power. Used correctly, it could possibly save the heavens from some mad man's folly. Paul didn't dare gamble on the outcome. He would educate himself and intervene swiftly if he deemed it necessary. If one man had to be in control of the system, then let it be him.

CHAPTER 12

Seven in the morning Paul glanced at his corn flakes to see if any were still floating. His spoon was cluttered with the soggy little devils. Most of them tried to hide beneath the milk's surface. He placed the spoon back in the bowl. It was going to be a coffee only morning he decided. The nightmares kept him awake half the night and he was just too exhausted to manage anything else for his growling stomach.

Helen came into the kitchen. Hair in place, make up on, and wearing a well pressed dress.

"Going shopping?" he asked.

"The boys need a few things for school." She took a container Diet powder out of the cupboard. She spooned some of the contents into a glass, added milk and began stirring the mixture. The elixir would keep her going until lunch. After she drank it down, she poured herself a cup of coffee and grabbed the sales section of the morning newspaper. Long ago he gave up trying to keep pace with her. Where she could, and usually did do a hundred things simultaneously, he could not. He barely managed enough organizational skills to complete a couple of belated household chores. Usually a marvel to watch, today the sight of her running back and forth made him only feel more depressed. Earlier, even the boys noticed he wasn't up to par. They said little to him as they made haste and left for school as soon as possible.

His facial expression said it all to Helen and she decided not to disturb him. After all, she reasoned, if she didn't get his full and undivided attention, then she probably would have better luck talking to the wall. When he looked this fired, he was useless. She refilled both of their cups of coffee and continued reading her newspaper adds. She hoped it wasn't finances that were bothering him. She knew it gave him ulcers and she hated it when they discussed money. She felt like she was being cornered; an economic prisoner.

He leaned back in his chair raising the front two legs up in the air. Something he did often in childhood and rarely as an adult. He pondered the tapes, Tim, the FBI, and the deranged former KGB agent. When the doorbell rang, he almost fell over along with the chair. Jolted to awareness, the thoughts vanished.

"Are you all right?" Helen gave him a concerned look and waited for him to reply. She never saw him startle before with such force, especially over something so trivial as a knock at the door. His nerves were on edge, but over what? At least it wasn't over finances, of that, she was certain. He never acted that way over money.

"I'm fine." He rose out of his chair in pain. His back muscles were in spasm half the night in response to the images.

"Would you like me to get that?" She asked noticing his discomfort.

"No, I have to wake up sometime." He rubbed his eyes one last time, rose from his chair, then lethargically made his way to the front door. As he opened the door a familiar figure greeted him.

"Mr. Crellin, can I have a word with you?" Special Agent Simson asked.

"What's the problem?" Paul yawned. He acted as if he could really care less.

"Looks like you had a rough night," Agent Simson said as he waited for Paul to invite him in. Simson was caring a small satchel that he thumped with his fingers in anticipation. Paul's warning lights were on. He had to be constantly on guard near this man. He wondered if he could stay on guard in such a sleepy state. Besides, there was a good possibility that even the best actor could not sound convincing before this man. Not knowing what he was up against, brevity would be his best defense. Simson was probably more cunning than a Lawyer and more skillful at dissection than a Surgeon.

And for what? He thought to himself. The longer he played the game, the further he implicated himself. He could confess all now and try and get off easy or it could get worse. But it wasn't as simple as that. If it was, Tim wouldn't have chosen him. He only analyzed programs: not the best choice for a comrade in the business of international conspiracy.

"We think Winters has flown the coop." The words resonated in Paul's ears and his thoughts shifted. "Do you know where he might have gone?"

"Who is it dear?" he heard Helen call out.

"It's nothing," he quickly assured her, hoping she would at least stay in the other room. "It's the FBI, they're trying to find someone from the office." He doubted she would leave it at that.

"Is that why the van was parked outside a few days ago?" She was standing right beside him.

"Ah yes mam," Simson replied. The authoritarian nature of her voice was too hard to resist. Paul looked at his wife as if to say stay back, then turned back to Simson.

"I haven't seen him."

"We thought he still might try and contact you. You did say he was going to meet you last night at Molly's?"

"That bar on Fifth Street?" Helen asked incredulously, but both men ignored her. What was her husband doing at a gay bar she thought to herself. She too felt Paul was acting odd lately, but this? She knew it had been awhile since they had shared any sexual intimacy, but she attributed that to age and more pressing matters. Since she herself rarely felt the need for making love, it was easy to set it aside, especially with their demanding schedules. It never occurred to her that Paul would seek out a place like that. She hoped she was just overreacting, she hoped to God she was.

"That's right," Paul answered. Christ, why did he have to bring it up in front of Helen? Then he saw it clearly; Simson was going to use her against him. She would be another tool for applying pressure on him. He felt the walls failing down around him.

"Did he say why?" Simson continued. The questions were the same as the ones he asked last night. Still, he found it torturous to answer them in front of his wife.

"No, that was it." He thought he was doing a good job keeping the answers short. He was determined to play this thing through a little longer. There was no room for mistakes. Finishing like Euripides, Simson the tragic talebearer, began to turn as if to leave, but stopped in mid-stride.

"By the way, he paged you over the phone, we think he knew the KGB was waiting for him." Helen's eyes grew wide and her mouth gaped open. Paul couldn't even guess how he would explain it all to her. Helen looked as if she was ready to go into shock.

"It's not what it sounds like. Let me talk to him alone. I'll give you all the details after he leaves." Paul put special emphasis on the last two words. He hoped this would reassure her, but he doubted it had the intended effect. She wasn't sure what to do actually, but the dissatisfied facial expressions the two men gave her warned her to let things rest for now. She acquiesced by going up stairs. She knew she could bide her time until she could corner him alone on the issue, but the suspense was killing her. Simson resumed the discussion in a hushed tone of voice.

"Now if I'm correct, and the agent you ran into last night is who we think he is, then Winters is involved in something over his head." He paused for effect. Paul's expression didn't waver. Undaunted, Simson remained stern and continued. "Now if I can prove he's involved in espionage, then he could get life in prison. That is of course if the Russians or whoever they are don't get to him first." Paul's head began to throb with pain. Was he playing the fool? Was he a patsy in a game where he could wind up the big loser? He rubbed his irritated eyes. Simson still could not determine if Paul was hiding anything. He felt he was far too removed to be involved in any existing espionage. He was a new employee and there was evidence of covert activities long before his arrival. Still, he was the last one to have contact with Timothy Winters, which brought him back to suspect number one. If he was involved, then he was one cool tomato Agent Simson thought.

"It used to be standard practice for the KGB to operate in pairs. Now the man you described moves around faster than we can catch him. His partner, however, may be a planted mole either at Wescon Industries or somewhere in the near vicinity. It would make my day to bust one of those boys, so do me a favor and see if you recognize anyone in these pictures." He pulled two dozen, eight by ten, and glossy black and whites from the side of the small brief case. Paul stood in the hallway and examined the photos.

Hospitality may have dictated that he formally invite Simson inside the house, but he had no intention of having him stay so long. He just wanted to look at the pictures and quickly send Agent Simson on his way. He proceeded to look through the stack at a good pace. He recognized no one. They were mostly telephoto shots. Enlarged to the point of almost being too grainy to discern details or way out of focus. The men wore drab suits regardless of whether they were sitting around a table or standing in the outdoors.

"They wear a lot of polyester don't they?" Paul stated trying to break the monotony. He already knew the answer. A few years ago he stayed in the town of Narita, Japan next to the New Tokyo International Airport. He stayed at the Hotel Centraza where, at the time, the Aeroflot crews laid over. It was his first actual encounter with KGB officials. They stood out in their poorly made polyester suits and synthetic black shoes. Their eyes were popping out of their heads as they walked through Daiei Department store, located adjacent to the hotel. This was way before Glasnost and Perestroika. They found the decadent displays overwhelming. They were accustomed to the long lines and little for sale. They examined every section of the store. One would look at the merchandise as if trying to find out what the catch was, while his comrade kept guard and surveyed the premises. Paul had never seen such neurotic behavior before, and that is exactly why he and the business people he was with followed the Russians around the store. Not too long of course, just long enough for the Russians to become suspicious. Then there was the time in Hong Kong too he thought. He was shopping with his wife when he heard two women conversing in Russian. When he looked over, he saw a mother and daughter in ill-fitting clothes that seemed to clash whenever possible. Ten feet behind them lingered a man in a stoic brown polyester suit. "Moscow's hands are long and dirty." It was a phrase he had read somewhere and the situation brought it back to mind; eyes and hands constantly hovering over the people. He heard that there were still some diehards in the new Russia that wanted to go back to the old ways: back to the good old days.

Back through the pictures he went. This time however, he stopped at a picture taken somewhere in the Sun Belt. Three men stood by the edge of a pool apparently discussing business while

several people, mostly females, splashed in the water. A tall blond
man was wearing the same-checkered sports jacket he wore the
night he smashed Paul's face into the bathroom wall. Under closer
scrutiny he appeared to be looking over the shoulder of one of the
gentlemen. Paul followed his line of sight, which focused on a
woman poised on a folding lounge chair. She was sitting up when
the picture was taken. Her tight fitting one-piece swimsuit
revealed every splendid curve of her body. She worked out. Her
muscles were solid, but not to the point of looking gross or
unnatural. She seemed to be returning the man's look with a
suggestive smile. The fact that her nipples appeared erect through
her swimsuit could have been merely coincidental, possibly due to
the ambient temperature, and not suggestive in nature. She held a
long stemmed glass as if to make a toast. She was indeed very
attractive. She reminded him of someone; someplace else. Then it
hit him.

"I sat next to her in the bar last night."

"Are you sure?" There was no emotion, just the question.

"Yes, I'm positive."

"Then Winters is a dead man," he said matter-of-factly. Paul
felt a lump growing in his throat. The way he said it scarred him
half to death.

"How do you know?" He choked the words out of his
mouth.

"They were waiting for him. These old Soviets don't wait for
anyone. They only went after you when they realized he gave
them the slip. Both of them used to be upper echelon KGB agents.
They aren't KGB anymore, as a matter of fact, we don't know who
they really work for now. Could be for another Soviet holdover
group, or even for another country. The woman is tagged to at
least a dozen deaths in this country alone; although all
circumstantial. Winters was probably supposed to give them
something and couldn't fulfill his end of the bargain. That's why
they asked you if he gave you anything. In my opinion, he's flown
and just like us, you're their only lead." Great, Paul thought. He
didn't want to think of the consequences.

"What can I do?" he finally mustered the nerve to ask.

"As long as they follow you discreetly, you'll know that Mr.
Winter is still alive. That's the way it usually works. And they

may want to talk to you again, so beware. We'll try and keep an eye out for them as best as we can. We'll put a man on your tail until things cool off, but the minute Winters tries to contact you, notify us immediately." Simson turned and looked over the landscape; a matter of habit. A nagging feeling kept interrupting his concentration.

"You sure you can't think of any reason why of all the people in the world, the last person he wanted to talk to was you?" It sounded more like a condemning statement than a question. It was just one more screw to be twisted in. One more attempt to find a weak spot.

"Not at all." He lied. He still found it hard to swallow.

"If that's true, then you and your family are probably safe from them." Each time he added a little more fear. Now he had entered the immediate family. It was a good way to make those easily frightened crack..

"What do you mean?" the words slipped out before Paul could stop them. Simson smiled, he was getting somewhere finally.

"These former KGB agents don't follow the same rules as we do. If they think they're warranted, they can be most unscrupulous. But, if you're clean, they are generally fair." His vernacular, as well his intonations were driving Paul up the wall. Probably, generally, usually, what kind of vague words were these? Simson was playing with him. This self-made Sherlock Homes suspected more than he wished to reveal.

"Have a nice day," Simson said as he turned and walked away. He loved to use this California phrase in a derogatory sense. Matter of fact, he liked using most phrases in a derogatory sense. Paul watched through the living room window as the blue van drove off. He decided right then not to go to work today. He would stay locked up in his study and search the tapes and find out what the hell was behind this turbulent mystery before it all blew up in his face: he only hoped he had enough time.

CHAPTER 13

It was Saturday morning, the day when his wife and son's slept in as late as possible. Not until noon would the noise emitted by normal household activities interrupt his concentration. Now was prime time to get something accomplished. So, early he rose and continued to sift through the contents of the tapes. He spent the time aimlessly wandering through the information. The groups of data were mere subsections of the master program, but for one human to review, they still represented a formidable task. So far, the two sentences in the note were the only clues to unraveling this mystery. None of his own guesses or hunches panned out. "Activate your interest," and "Highly critical." In Tim's mind they may have been deemed good clues, but each disk contained some two hundred megabytes of information and the task of searching through the data seemed more difficult than finding a good pizza in China. A real formidable task and something might get overlooked when monotony set in.

Earlier, he concluded one tape dealt with security. If Tim needed his help, then it must have had something to do with altering or correcting the existing data. After all, that's what he did best. Which meant he would have to breach security to perform whatever task was necessary. He assumed that the remainder of the second tape was devoted to helping him solve this aspect. Therefore, he concluded the second tape contained the sections that needed revisions. This was the logical process he followed.

It was also the only approach to the problem he could come up with.

He separated the material into several distinct categories from which to search. With this step completed the most confronting problem was where to begin. He arbitrarily picked a section that held some promise.

"Here we go." He whispered to himself. He uncovered a subsection on systems activation. If this was truly the right section, then the worst part was already over. He had been so frustrated and all the time he couldn't help but wonder why Tim was so vague. Better yet, why couldn't he tell him face to face what the problem was ... like the day he came to the house? Paul heard a knock on the door and the thoughts passed. A shot of adrenaline soared through his body as he shoved the tapes into his top desk drawer.

"Yes," he sounded out hesitantly.

"Are you busy?" Helen announced a split second before she entered the room. Opening the door she caught him in the midst of darkening the monitor. A clear sign he was trying to hide something. She didn't no whether to think it had something to do with the FBI or if it was just part of his normal paranoia. He could be real strange at times. Especially when left inside the confines of his study. At least there was one part of him that was still functioning normally. She recalled the last night's passionate romance. It had been missing for quite some time, but at least the questions raised by his visit to Molly's bar had been laid to rest. She was quite satisfied that she could still stir the fire within him.

"You planning on staying in there all day?" She asked. "Time to pay the price for playing all day." She smiled then left, leaving the study door open.

"Good morning," was all he could muster. She already knew he was up to something, she could tell. She could read him like a book. He could also tell from the phrase she used he was in for a full day's worth of chores and that there was little chance or escape until they were completed. She felt it was her responsibility to drag him out into the open, to see his sons, and to be part of the family.

He spent the rest of the day trying to get back to the tapes. His life became busy from the moment the children were conceived and the pace had only quickened over the years. He enjoyed his family; it was just natural for a male to complain. The thought of changing his lifestyle seldom entered his mind. Especially with Helen's sudden renewed interest in sex. God, what a woman he thought. The last few days he thought about his family a great deal. The longer he possessed the tapes, the more conscience he became of their well-being.

He was physically exhausted by the time he re-entered his study. Helen's list of things to do was endless. Only by eating twice his normal amount at dinner was he able to gain enough strength to face his arduous undertaking. Line by line he scrutinized the files. By midnight he decided to give up. He examined some several thousand lines of information and felt lost in a sea of alphabetic entries. Never the less, even with this brief survey, he had come across several areas where subtle changes could have made the existing program more precise; but this was not his concern. Moving further through the data he found another lengthy loop that appeared to be poorly organized. He yawned and with some degree of disappointment he decided to call it quits. How could anyone rely on a set of commands so heavily flawed and expect the program to accurately function on the first pass? Through the grapevine he heard the entire program consisted of some seven million subsections of information. If he could find fault within a few thousand lines, then the overall number of errors must be staggering. If even one percent of the glitches lead to an over all shut down, then the SDI program was doomed. He could visualize billions worth of hardware orbiting uselessly around the earth. Maybe he was just being too cynical. Just because they didn't meet his standards, didn't mean the faults couldn't be eventually ironed out and the program completed. Paul took one last look at the screen then turned off the computer. It was time to get a Gin and Tonic and forget about this mass of binomial garble if he could.

CHAPTER 14

When the computer shut down he faintly heard noises emitted by the television in the living room. He wondered who was still awake at this hour? He knew it had to be one of his sons, for Helen rarely stayed up this late. She must have been exhausted this evening, for she didn't even come into the study and kiss him good night. He quietly cracked open the door to his study. A large devious grin crossed his face. There, lying on the couch was his son Philip. Philip's most recent girlfriend was practically wrapped around his body. Hair was tossed and tangled. Their clothes were slightly disarrayed. Philip's hands were up under her shirt. His eyes opened wide in shock when he opened them only to see his dad coming out of his office.

"What are you watching?" Paul asked trying not to burst out with laughter. The girl's long blonde hair concealed most of the redness in her face. Both of them rose to sit up while trying to inconspicuously adjust their clothing. Philip was mad for having been caught so completely off guard. For the girl, the situation became even more embarrassing when she realized that her bra had been unsnapped in the back and there was no way to rectify the situation discretely. Damn Philip she thought. He always tried to take things a little too far, but boy was he a good kisser. All he had to do was touch her and she tingled all over. She only hoped that he liked her, as much as she liked him. After all, he was a sophomore and she was a freshman. She had just been a little more physically developed for her age and not only was she thankful, but well aware that her attributes had helped her gain the recognition of this handsome sophomore. The rest of her friends were envious. She was the talk of her social click. If only he wasn't so forward.

"We are, Ah... I thought you and mom went to bed already."

"No, I've been in the study." The room was dim. The lamp was on low. He spotted a big bowl of popcorn on the end table and made his way towards it. "Do you mind if I help myself to the popcorn?" He reached in and scooped up a handful of the mildly warmed kernels.

"Ugh, go ahead dad," came an uneasy response. Philip's throat became dry just like his dad's when he became nervous and it delayed his ability to speak. He had forgotten all about the popcorn the minute he and Julie sat on the couch. Damn he thought. He was doing so well until his father ruined everything. He had planned and dreamed about this evening all week. Then his thoughts turned to anguish as he realized that he was in for it now. He could already see his father telling his brother how he caught them making out on the couch. If his brother found out, he wouldn't be able to live it down for a week. Then he looked at Julie and decided it had been worth the risk. At first she just blushed with guilt, but now she was glaring at Philip as she straightened her shirt and turned to face the television. Philip had never seen a girl get so mad at him, and yet, it gave her a quality reminiscent of his mother. This girl could hold her own and was not to be taken lightly. This girl was special. So how would he make it up to her? Paul could feel the tension building so he decided to leave the room for a moment.

"I think I'll get something to drink," he said as he grabbed another handful.

"You said they were asleep." He heard Julie angrily whisper to Philip as he took his time in the kitchen. Eating the popcorn was all he could do to keep from laughing. He slowly poured himself a gin and tonic then came back into the living room. This time both of them had their hair back in place and the pillows were re-arranged. He nonchalantly sat down in his favorite chair and reached for another handful of popcorn.

"Well Dad, we have to go."

"Oh, you have to leave so soon?" A mixed expression hung on his son's face.

"Yeah, we didn't know it was so late already."

"I guess you can loose track of time watching TV." Philip gave him a dirty look. He knew what his father was insinuating. One couldn't help grow up in this household without being able to read between the lines. He stretched out his hand and motioned for Julie to stand up.

"It was nice seeing you again Mr. Crellin," she said passively. Her eyes barely met his for a fraction of a second then back down to the floor as she began to blush again.

"Good by," Paul sounded out as the front door closed. Now he had not only obtained the front room for himself, but a big bowl of popcorn too!

As he sat eating away, he recalled earlier times when he dated his wife and how some things seemed to repeat themselves over and over again with each succeeding generation.

"Here's to hormones," he raised his glass and toasted. He then reached his hand back inside the bowl. The kernels were still warm.

CHAPTER 15

Philip entered the house as quietly as possible. He managed to patch things up with Julie after that embarrassing incident with his father, and now he wished only to sleep. He shut the front door and turned to find his father, who had probably finished three Gin and tonics before he fell fast asleep in his chair.

"Dad, don't you think you ought to go to bed?" Philip said as he shook his father's shoulder.

"What?" Paul answered as he forced his eyes to open. He focused on the television while trying to collect his thoughts.

"Where's your brother?" He asked half asleep.

"He's staying at a friend's house."

"Her parents know about it?" He was tired, but not brain dead and asleep.

"No Dad, he and some of his friends are having a party."

"Last time he and some of his friends had a party, he was sick the next day and he complained of spoiled Kool-Aid." Paul said the words rather sarcastically.

"I know Dad," Philip said with glee. "That's why I stopped at the store to get some bacon." Philip held up a brown paper bag. He had a mischievous smile on his face. Paul failed to make the connection. "I figured the smell of burnt bacon in the morning would make him get even sicker." He was beaming ear to ear.

"You'd do that to your own brother?" Paul asked trying to cast doubt on his son's actions.

"He borrows my stuff then breaks it. If this was Singapore, I'd let'em cane him!"

"Does your mother know about this party?"

"Yes," he replied matter-of-factly. Then with the thought of 'Dad get real,' he added, "Dad did you expect him to ask you if he could go out and get drunk with his friends?"

"What did he ask your mother?"

"I don't know, but mom's easier."

"Not when I ask," Paul whispered to himself. They both fell silent for a few moments while he gained enough awareness to pull himself away from his chair.

"I guess its time to go to bed." He yawned one final time then stood up. Several pieces of popcorn fell from his shirt onto the carpet. Both he and his son reached down to pick them up. Philip knew his mom would come after him first if the living room was left a mess. After all, she watched him make the stuff. And he only did that to have something to do until his mom went to bed.

"What were you doing up so late?" his son asked.

"Nothing." He picked up the last kernel then raised up. "That's one of the few joys of being a parent. You don't have to answer to anyone." Then in after thought,

"Except your mom." They both remained quiet while they picked up and cleaned the rest of the room. Philip put his bacon away in the refrigerator. He couldn't wait to wake his brother up at the first sign of light.

"By the way, how did you make out with your girlfriend?" Philip ignored the implied double meaning. "I mean is she still upset over being caught off guard like that?"

"Yeah, Julie's fine," he shrugged his shoulders and said. He realized he made a double meaning of his own and felt ecstatic inside, for she was more than fine, but he didn't want his father to know. He hated those sex lectures.

Paul could smell the perfume emanating from his son's shirt. "You're lucky it wasn't your mother who walked in on you?"

"We were only kissing."

"That's only because I interrupted the mood."

"We weren't going to do anything." Philip decided to take a strong stand even if he had to bend the truth slightly. His father just didn't understand sometimes. He wondered if his father saw him with his hand in her shirt. He should have kept his eyes open while kissing her. There was no telling how long his father stood there or what he saw.

"Right." Paul rolled his eyes. "And there isn't a world population problem either." They both made their way upstairs without further comment. "See you in the morning Philip, and by the way, I won't mention it if you don't." He smiled at his son then entered his Helen's bedroom. He knew it was one promise he wouldn't have to keep long, for Philip would tell his brother Henry all about his date it in the morning. Leaving out, of course, the last part where he got caught in the act of exploration. Brotherhood rivalry knew no bounds of decency.

Helen was fast asleep. Paul's clothes thudding against the floor had no ill effect. Carefully slipping into bed, so as not disturb her, he too fell fast asleep. But with mystery to solve, he restlessly woke up several times during the night. At five in the morning he finally capitulated. He put on a robe and went down to his study. Something he had seen in the program was gnawing at him. He couldn't put his finger on it, but he knew it had something to do with a strange loop in one particular subsection; two hundred lines or so, redundantly sending commands. He wasn't exactly sure what the commands were for, but he had seen almost identical commands hours before in another subsection. To rest his curiosity, he had to go back down stairs and take a closer look.

"There it is," he said to himself as he peered at the screen. He began to read in earnest each of the one hundred and thirty two lines. "Jesus Christ." Paul gasped and shook his head. He didn't know who was responsible, but someone had inserted this loop to bypass the entire defense network. These few well-placed commands essentially negated the other seven million lines of information. They ordered a defense satellite to ignore the presence of a projectile that emitted a signal at a certain frequency. In this instance, a missile broadcasting an alternating signal between a few hundred thousand hertz could essentially pass right through the defense screen. The question was which side devised this monstrous side step? He doubted Tim wrote it for the Russians. After all, if they had instructed him on what frequency to use, then they would already have a copy of this information in their possession. The fact that he was supposed to hand over this tape negated this train of logic. Unless, he considered, they didn't trust him and wanted a hard copy for verification, but then again, that would be too risky. Better to just leave it be. Could Tim have had second thoughts? The Russians were expecting him to deliver something. Or could it have been that he stumbled across this piece of program by chance, was going to sell it to the Russians, and then got cold feet at the last moment. This would explain his disappearance. But why give it to him?

He spent the rest of the day pondering these questions. The biggest of all, was what he was going to do with the information. One thing was certain; he was going to become deeply involved in the programming of the SDI satellites. There was just too much at stake to leave in the hands of others less adroit. Errors could destroy billions worth of property, but with this, one determined man could insert commands that could devastate entire nations. Having gained access, his next step would be to counter any such subsystem with a few of his own well placed, and especially well concealed, commands.

CHAPTER 16

It was Wednesday morning, slumpday, as it was so affectionately called by the employees of Wescon Industries. Two days down and forgotten; two more miserable days of the week left to some how get through. Still no sign of Timothy Winters. Paul handed in his application to work on the SDI executive committee Monday morning and couldn't wait to get started. Last week he would have thought anyone mad to approach him with such a job offer, but a lot can change overnight with the right inducement.

Today just might be the day he'd receive his confirmation. A strange feeling of excitement swirled inside him. The only obstacle in his way was his own past attitudes concerning the SDI program. He made no beefs about where he stood on this issue even as late as last week. A dove to a hawk overnight might make them just a little too wary. He hoped his reputation, as one of the top analysts would compensate for his past political disposition. He sat at his desk peering into the screen. Unable to concentrate, he looked at the data while his thoughts drifted to other subjects.

"Dr. Crellin, can I have a word with you?" It was the amiable General himself speaking. Seldom seen around the working areas, he always reappeared when things were about to happen. His voice sounded gruff, but probably as sincere as the man could muster at the present moment. Paul started and came to a loose form of attention. The effect gave the General a twisted sense of pleasure. He genuinely loved these unexpected visits, it reminded him of unannounced inspections of the old days. They may not stand up and give a smart salute like they did in the military, but just to see civilians shake from surprise was well worth it. Wearing his ever-present smile, he entered and closed the door behind him. He examined the office as if for the very first time. He felt claustrophobic in the tiny confines. He would make this brief as possible.

"I received your application to change departments." He walked over to Paul's desk and brushed his fingers against it. Old habits were hard to give up and he did enjoy the pomposity of a good inspection. He also believed a mock inspection of this type left a person more humbled and more insecure. Paul thought the man was crazy. It was a view he recently discovered that was widely held many of his peers. "I read your requisition," he continued. "You want to tell me what changed your mind?"

"To be honest," Paul looked at him as sincerely as he could, "Money". I think you know what happened to my company, and there isn't a lot of time left to start over saving for retirement." He paused as if reflecting on past events. "I could have said 'in the interest of my country', but you wanted the truth." He sat back down in his chair, folded his arms, and stared into the General's eyes. Moorehouse stood still for a brief moment as he evaluated each word. Abruptly he held out his right hand.

"You're going to get an increase in pay as a position in your new department deserves. And along with fortune, if you prove yourself, you'll get fame as well." His smile broadened wider than Paul had ever thought possible. Maybe it was brought about by the concurrence of greed. Maybe the General sincerely meant his welcoming him into the fellowship of Wescon. Either way, Paul felt moved by Moorehouse's mere presence.

"When do I start?" he finally broke the silence.

"The first of next week. I'll turn your current post... I mean project, over to Doug Sanborn. You can take a vacation in the meantime." Paul immediately had visions of several leisure days.

"I like the job already," he said and smiled. The General was ecstatic. Patience had rewarded him with one of the best think tanks in the country. He personally had secured the employment of five top scientists for Wescon Industries. Feeling magnanimous he added, "In this company, if you play ball and keep your nose clean, then your going to go far. Oh, and there are no other games in town." He paused for a moment as if to listen for the echo of his own words. " I think your going to do all right."

"Thank you sir." His words were vibrant, he felt disgusted.

"Not at all. See you bright and early next week."
Moorehouse left the room slamming the door shut behind him. He came in like a blizzard, he went out like a tornado. Paul took a

deep breath and leaned further back in his chair. Part of him felt like vomiting in disgust, while the other side reveled with joy. There was nothing like working from the inside, he thought to himself. Maybe he could make a good double agent? No, thoughts like that would only get him into trouble, but how much trouble?

CHAPTER 17

Three years passed quickly without incident since he first gained entrance into the SDI programming department. Both sons had left for college and the house had once again become a temple filled with peace and solitude. Timothy Winters was still listed as missing and presumed to be dead. This always stuck in the back of Paul's mind due to the precarious position Tim had left him in. One thing was sure, the batch file subsections Tim gave him years ago never crossed his path through standard company channels. It either meant the files were restricted to others eyes only whom he didn't know, and they existed only on a handful of tapes, or the files really didn't exist at all. He didn't really wholeheartedly believe this last assumption. In a company like Wescon Industries, who was entrenched in covert activities as the media depicted in past events, nothing could be ruled out. All he could be sure of, as one of the existing senior advisors in the department was that the contingencies mandated in the tapes were not a current topic, and that was about it. On the other hand, if the company wasn't hiding anything from him, then the only area in doubt was Tim's association with the former Soviets. The simplest assertion being that he had been contracted by some renegade former KGB agent to insert subsections into the overall program. If this was the case, he had an easy task, for an insertion between seven million or more lines of data might never be noticed until too late. But, if this was his task, then why didn't he just do it and get it over with? Why spend countless hours devising the loophole of the century, just to back out the very instant before implementation? It made little sense. There had to be another angle he hadn't thought of or one he'd overlooked. Maybe he had become too exasperated with the entire situation and couldn't muster a true investigator's insight.

Three years these thoughts rolled around in his head. All pertinent details he had stored away on single floppy disks. This way, if he was ever found missing, at least his family could learn the background behind his current reasoning. Being a scientist working to create better military weapons had divided the family and cost him his relationship with his oldest son Henry. Even Philip, who was studying computer science at Cal Poly Tech, found it hard to accept his dad's occupation. It went directly against the way they were raised. It reminded him again of an infamous phrase:

"The danger is, that politicians will accept as inevitable the destruction of innocent people to achieve their goals and that scientists will concentrate on the means, and ignore the ends of their research."

He couldn't be sure if he remembered it correctly. It was taken from a speech President Roosevelt was going to give on Jefferson day, but died before giving it. He repeated the phrase so many times to his son's that they had memorized it. He had always believed that to watch a war movie without this thought in the back of your mind, led to passive participation instead of critical contemplation. The passage embodied one of his family's deepest moral beliefs. Never the less, he felt compelled to oversee the development of SDI. The irony in all of this was that his past encounters with the FBI helped to arouse an interest in this institution by his younger son Philip as a future employee. What a turn about in a generation's ideology he thought. Of course, even he and his sixties colleagues with backgrounds in government distrust had grown to acknowledge the FBI's vital role in the nation's security.

What the cost had been to Helen was another tender subject. Most of their former close friends were considered doves. Actually, they were just democrats soft on military spending. The problem was, he was perceived as one of the chief republican hawks and although she still tried to socialize with them, the topic of conversation eventually led to a political debate where chastising remarks and haughty innuendoes soon prevailed. At times they could be so cruel he thought. He would have liked to help her out. Tell her more about what he actually did, so she could help defend his position, but it was too dangerous to confide in her: for her own safety, if for nothing else. His only consolation was that the time was close at hand when peacekeeper satellites would be orbiting safely in space and he could move on to other subjects. Even now, as he stood in the middle of mission control in Houston, he reflected upon what he lost against what he had gained. There was virtually no time or place safe from his own self-criticism. Looking at a huge television screen he watched as a rocket bellowed out smoke in preparation for launch. Many would have reveled in their success, but how could he feel like a proud technological father when the outcome had cost him the alienation of his family? He forced himself to appear happy, then turned to acknowledge those standing near him. He and a select few had the honor to witness the placement in orbit, and soon the initial test of the first prototype Laser Battle Station, "LBS", as it was now called most frequently called. The old Star Wars name had already gone out of political favor. The emergence of super conducting magnetic storage devices made the potential for space-based lasers a reality. Therefore, the new buzzword had to reflect the more narrowed direction the Defense Initiative Project was taking. Even the word defense had been dropped from the satellite's name, for the scuttlebutt was that the next generation could have earthbound offensive abilities as well. This was a prospect that he would have to fight to prevent. It was also something that made both the Russians and Chinese quite apprehensive, and with heightened tensions came the possibility for global mistakes. But, by this stage of the game there was no turning back. The United States was committed and so was he. The actual battle star itself had been launched the previous day without incident. Another large screen on the forward facing wall monitored its progress. Red lines represented its course since liftoff.

"Ladies and gentlemen, in a very few moments we will begin the test." Paul along with several others waited impatiently as the countdown formality began. Where the sound of the Texan voice was coming from he had no idea.

"Ten, nine, eight." This was the first of a two part series. It was just a dummy ballistic missile being launched.

"Seven, six, five." In this exercise, the object was for the prototype to recognize the missile as a threat and neutralize the missile during its boost phase.

"Four, three, two, one!" A sudden hush fell upon them, followed by a great roar as the mighty engine ignited.

"We have lift off. The clock is running." For almost two minutes all personnel froze, eyes glued to the screen. A small dot arched upward on the screen towards the heavens. In real time, the ballistic missile would have been on its way to somewhere deep within the Soviet Union. One minute the red dot on the accompanying screen flashed brightly as it ascended; the next minute it vanished. Over sixty people simultaneously broke out cheering and reveling in their accomplishment, then quickly settled back down to work. They would still have to narrow down the time from launch recognition to impact by at least thirty seconds. They didn't dare give multiple tipped nuclear missiles the chance to disperse warheads and seek individual targets before securing the verification and acquisition phase of the launch.

The next phase was about to begin. This time, the destination of the missile would be the battle star itself. The situation being exemplified was whether or not the prototype could defend itself as well as it defends the nation that built it. The prototype would have two approaches to overcome this problem. It could either move to a higher orbit in order to avoid damage by nuclear explosion, or it could fire a so-called smart rock and essentially attack and destroy the incoming warhead. What the prototype decided in the next few minutes would have devastating economical repercussions for the LBS-SDI program.

The count down finished; the missile was off. A bright blue dot worked its way up the screen towards a green dot. Around the LBS, (the green dot), was a thin red lit circle. Had the engine on the missile been slightly larger, the prototype could have recognized it as ballistic missile and already destroyed it by laser, but the small size registered as being non-nuclear in origin. The missile quickly reached this critical penetration zone. The prototype now had to decide whether it was on a collision course and whether to run or fight. A millionth of a second passed, the choice was made. Out from one of sixty-four clustered tubes a small seven-pound metal terminal seeker launched. The metal bullet sent forth a wave signal as it crossed the rarefied atmosphere at a phenomenal speed of 17,000 miles per hour. The incoming missile involuntarily responded, relaying a stream of data back to mission control. The smart rock also sent a detailed stream of data. Both streams of information would later be analyzed back at

Houston. With the smart rock's lock on response engaged, it adjusted its internal guidance system. The maneuvering thrusters sparked to life and within a thin fraction of time, the smart rock impacted against the aggressor and rendered it harmless.

A deep gash ran down the length of the slightly deformed and twisted missile. The impotent piece of space debris was left was left to wander aimlessly or burn up during re-entry into earth's atmosphere. The blue dot on the screen vanished.

"The project's a success," he heard someone announce over the roar of clapping and cheering. Further modifications would add on several hundred more smart rocks to each side of every LBS station. This was a process similar to attaching a child's' Lego blocks to one another. With a belt driven feeder mechanism, the Smart rocks could be discharged at a phenomenal rate, similar to automatic weapon fire. Plus, the entire process could be solely regulated by artificial computer intelligence. It was almost assured that within the next four years, half a dozen LBS stations would be hovering in the heavens. How this technology would be used remained Paul's greatest concern and nemesis.

CHAPTER 18

Six months prior to the failed coup against Gorbechev on August 19, 1991, Georgi Mihailovich Malenkov, Secretary of the Soviet Committee of State Security (KGB), looked out his one-way viewing window at Red Square. The weather was getting cold, but no snow was predicted for the next few days. Still, he decided to walk through the underground tunnel system to the main cabinet meeting. With his monogrammed handkerchief he bought in Zurich, he wiped the beads of perspiration from his forehead. The water molecules would turn to ice crystals upon contact with the air on such a bright sunny Moscow day. He put on his overcoat and adjusted his party pin on his left lapel of his British tailored gray suit. He was one of the privileged in this impoverished worker's paradise. He only wondered how long his good fortune would last. A knock came on his door. It wasn't his usual escort, but a man he was most anxious to see.

"Come in," he said with a thick Georgian accent. Georgi's voice reminded the young man of Stalin. It caused the young man to stop and reexamine the man in front of him. Georgi Malenkov often had this affect on people. It helped make them uneasy in his presence. They felt weary about his connections and ultimately his political power. As a trained member of the GRU, the young Captain composed himself quickly. He was a personal aid to General Andrei Nikolai Petrovich, Secretary of the Glavnoye Razvedivateinoe Upravienie (Military Intelligence Service).

"Well?" Malenkov was barely able to ask. His throat was too dry to spit out anything more. He was very nervous. He had never been so unsure of himself in the last five years. It seemed everything was projected for five year cycles in this topsy-turvy social order.

"Your demands have been met Comrade Malenkov," the captain said unenthusiastically.

"And my son?"

"His grades were not sufficient for entry, we had to adjust them. It took time, but all has been arranged." It was Malenkov's golden parachute. He would retain his dying party's privileges; his dacha (summer home) on the Baltic Sea, and to the satisfaction of his lovely wife Nina, their pathetic example of an overindulged offspring would be enrolled in the University of Leningrad. With a little luck he might pass his way through something simple, like modern Russian studies. His wife, Yevonka, would finally be satisfied. All he had to do was retire early. He halfheartedly tried to smile as he picked up the papers on his desk.

"Let us not keep them waiting." Georgi said as he raised his arms in a gesture as if to say out of my hands. The two men left the inner office and were escorted by two KGB field agents.

Right on time they were ushered into one of the many similar styled cabinet chambers. All rooms looked the same. All had a worn out red carpets that still smelled from the original glue used to hold together the weaving to the floor. The walls were pale yellow, just like the rest of the miserable city. On one wall stood the stoic portrait of Lenin. Muscovites couldn't decorate a cemetery he thought to himself. Perestroika was new to Moscow, it had always been the way of life on the other side of the Caucasus mountains. To return to his southern colorful city of Tbilisi would be a banishment he could live with.

"Good afternoon General Secretary," he said as he entered the room. The aids and GRU captain stopped outside the door to the room.

"You have something important to tell the committee?" The General Secretary prompted him.

"Yes, I am submitting my resignation papers." He handed the General Secretary his papers and stood behind his assigned chair. There was no reason to sit for he would not be staying long. As the General Secretary examined the papers he looked down at the empty chair and then over to General Petrovich. Andrie had already told him whom to name as his successor. The name was listed in the papers. All that needed to be done was to ratify the new appointment. Andrei's repugnant face crinkled into a devilish grin. Of course he was in a position to smile all he wanted. With the naming of that spineless twit to the head of the KGB, the first main directorate of the KGB would become a vassal of the second main directorate of the soviet army general staff. Andrei now held more power than any other man in the USSR without a coupe. And if he could keep his followers in line, Andrei could put Glasnost back on the shelf along with Marxist ideology, and stow them away in Lenin's tomb, or at least derail them for a few precious years until he'd lined his own pockets.

Poor man Andrei thought. His agents almost bungled operation Ozyera Duxhi (lake spirits) and now he would be held accountable. The operation to spirit away a top American computer engineer was too critical to demand anything less.

"And what is the situation at this time with the operation Duxhi?" the General Secretary's voice bellowed out. He wanted it expressly known that he was not happy. Georgi tried to steady himself. This powerful faction of the central committee had still not ruled out his own execution.

"With the General Secretaries permission," General Petrovich interrupted. The General Secretary nodded in his direction. He felt Andrei's power and couldn't deny Him rushing to Georgi's assistance.

"Georgi and I have already set up another operative inside Wescon Industries. A man very high up. We've determined he's reliable, and worth billions of rubles in information. We'll be contacting a secondary source within days." The news astounded the small group of men, but no one more than Georgi himself. He couldn't believe the generosity of his victor. He not only called him by his first name without his title preface, but in addition, he shared the achievement of a successful KGB operation. Petrovich was more complex than he first thought.

Petrovich helped spare Georgi, so he could use him later. After saving him, Georgi would always be in his debt. Petrovich smiled at his new friend and ally. Georgi could not help but reply with an expression of the same falsehood. The General Secretary was satisfied. They all shook hands with Georgi, said their farewells, and he left the room as a simple Soviet citizen, albeit a privileged one. To still be alive was the greatest privilege they could bestow upon him.

CHAPTER 19

Sunday morning the new director of research and development for Wescon Industries could afford to take it easy. In just twelve short years he had worked his way up to the top. Presently making over two hundred thousand dollars a year, he had cut his work hours in half and had an army of lesser paid-overworked individuals to do his bidding. He was essentially living the life of every capitalists dream. Yet, he was still troubled by what should have been his most enjoyable period in life. He was still plagued by the image of the SDI program and the feeling if he was not careful, he could be held responsible for a global catastrophic event. Although in some ways the idea seemed far fetched with the world's apparent movement towards global disarmament. Never the less, this was just one side of the coin. On the other side, his position gave him hands on use and knowledge of the latest LBS developments. He could in effect, personally decide what would be the fate of the entire project, or so he thought. He could, at the least, either improve the system, or destroy it by the insertion of a few well-placed bits of coded information. It was the power that made it all worthwhile. Manipulation of a system this complex was officially thought impossible by most experts outside of Wescon Industries. This is the impression Paul gave and wanted to give. He portrayed the perfect stoic hawk with total confidence. In his opinion, it was the responsibility of the masses to publicly denounce SDI or any other arms build up program. If they could affect its rate of progress, then his intervention might not be required. He could just sit back and provide an inside backup plan in case all else failed.

Even life at home had become easier to live with. His sons, both doves when it came to the arms race, never came to grips with their father's occupation. Because of this, they seldom kept in contact. Henry married and moved to Alaska, Philip was back east in graduate school and he already had a quasi-position working for the FBI part-time. The distance between them only further aggravated the situation.

Helen always seemed to remain in close contact with the kids no matter what. But she too had changed. She began to behave like the other Pentagon housewives. Money seemed no object for families of Generals and diplomats. Most activities were expected to be gratis, and with all of these prearranged functions, there was even less time to spend together. He found that even with his stipend salary, he was quickly running out of money without a wife close by to account for what happened to their bank reserves. At times he wondered where his life was leading him. Another pay increase could put him in the poorhouse.

Some of the privileges he now took for granted were a gross misuse of public funds. Just a few years ago such things he would have found disgusting. One instance in particular always came back to bother his conscience. Last year he and Helen went to Bermuda. For two weeks they stayed at a luxury hotel unofficially subsidized by the US government and they paid a token forty-two dollars a day for room and food. Their bar bill alone should have approached their monthly mortgage payment at such a ritzy resort. The French and Haitian cuisine was priceless. To top it all, the entire trip from airfare, etc., was tax deductible: a top-secret business trip of national interests. He failed to see where business entered into it, but he could see why the Pentagon wanted to keep it top secret. The trip planned for the Philippines this year would probably end the same way. In all, the life style except for the over indulgence in alcohol, wasn't bad. He just couldn't determine if it was slightly dishonest or outright immoral. Like most of his comrades, his personal convictions were being tested, and broken down, piece by piece, layer by layer.

He lay in bed an extra hour this morning. The previous week was filled with a strange buildup of activity and the events had left him exhausted. He met with General after General, Senator after Senator: each one demanding their own private tour; those with less rank or time in office compensated by asking more questions. The first wave of three fully functional battle satellites was scheduled for liftoff next Friday. The dignitary procession was just the government's way of reassuring itself that everything was ready, or so he thought.

Over the past year the three current space shuttles, one more at standby, had been flying all assignments with only a few hours or days between liftoff. It took only one flight to send up an LBS platform, but several more flights to install the racks of smart rocks and test all the equipment. The global weather pattern during that period seemed extremely disrupted. As if every entry or exit through the earth's atmosphere precipitated a major storm, tornado, or hurricane. Local crackpots and zealots aware of this disturbance pattern, played on it as a sign from God to stop whatever they were doing up there. The scheduled flights proceeded unabated. The flights would last a couple of days while they deployed their cargo and descended back down to earth. The rotated crews took two or three weeks off, then went back up again. NASA proved they could save money this way. A small full time staff aided by the military when extra manpower was needed, left more funds for other less militarily inclined projects. Some people saw this in the long term as nothing more than a deception on the part of the military to sweep NASA permanently under its' wing. Ironically, the freed up resources had actually enlarged NASA's role in the civilian sector: a role that had been diminishing over the last twenty years. In the short term, others saw the use of the military as a way to conceal things from the general public. One accusation in particular was unknowingly close to the truth. Using the military, a mass deployment of killer satellites could be effected and once up there, it would be too late to protest. At first Paul thought that each launch of three shuttles was the end to peace in space, but after a year of this periodic and repetitive cycle, even he became indifferent to their frequent liftoffs.

Paul stretched his limbs and yawned one final time. The house seemed unbearably quiet. Then he remembered that Helen had gone out with her friends for the day. The house was his to do with as he pleased. He wouldn't see her until six in the evening when the two of them were supposed to attend a diplomatic banquet. He attended several of these so-called banquets over the past four months. Elections were right around the comer. As usual, the company would reimburse him for the cost of the affair plus a little extra. Helen would get a chance to wear a new dress, enter the upper-social circle, and the candidate in question could add the proceeds of the get-together to his campaign war chest. It was anticipated that the candidate would reciprocate by favoring Wescon Industries sometime in the near future. Although the affair was made to look legal, several years ago, Paul would have found the whole charade disgusting. Now it was just part of the motions. Still, for his position of power, he considered his level of corruption minimal. That was something to feel good about.

Time for a shot of coffee he thought to himself. He never did get used to not having the boys messing around in the kitchen and even today the clean, quiet, surroundings saddened him. Once the battle stars were deployed, he was planning to officially quit. Maybe then, his sons would understand his position and they could grow closer together again.

Paul made himself a quick cup of coffee and headed for his favorite chair. The smell of the coffee was refreshing, but the taste was absolutely nauseating: that was the problem with instant coffee. Adding milk to the concoction didn't help much. The powdered caffeine coated crystals rose to the surface. All he could do now was drink it anyway, and wait for the caffeine to take its effect. Meanwhile, he spent the next few moments pondering what he would do for the remainder of the day. There were the lawn related chores, but he could put those off for another week before Helen would remind him. He could reshuffle papers in his study. He could check the oil level in his car. As of lately, the engine sounded terrible. The metal parts ticked and clicked like a loud clock about to run out of time. In fact, the more he thought about it, the more the list of things needing urgent attention grew. There was only one thing to do, he decisively concluded. He picked up the remote control box and turned on the television. Eight hours of viewing, then he could call it a day.

He swiftly turned the channels until he found an old western playing. The kind where the Indians had light skinned hands and dark red faces. The hats never fell off and worst of all was how they portrayed the Indian nation: A bunch of wild heathens bent on war. No wait a minute, he thought, that sounded like him and his co-workers. Anyway, it didn't really matter, it would take another sixty years before the white man would finally admit that four hundred to over a thousand years ago, great aboriginal Indian nations had existed across most of North America. Cultures that studied astronomy, smelted copper, had extensive trade with South America, and most important of all, highly structured religious and social systems. Many of which put the European cultures to shame. Yet, might is right and the Cavalry, dressed with white gloves and shinny swords, sent in to protect the land grabbers had an image hard to tarnish. Maybe that's why they still wore white lab coats with the Wescon insignia above the left pen pocket? He remembered seeing the movie years ago when he was just a kid, but he had forgotten the plot. It may have seemed like a drama then, but now it looked more like a play on the portrayal of his own life. The half-naked Indians were loosing their shirts for all their efforts.

After watching the demise of several lower budget Italian actors he decided to get something to eat. He was disgusted with the whole affair. The last Indian killed was especially pathetic. His face and hands matched in color, but white ankles showed beneath his deerskin pants: obviously from a northern tribe. It was nothing like the original movie, "Geronimo". That was his favorite. In that movie, the Indians were the good guys. Geronimo, played by Chuck Connors, was inspiring to watch in action; even if he was the only blue-eyed Indian in the movie.

Rummaging in the kitchen he found ten boxes of macaroni and cheese and little else. His wife was still buying some items as if the boys were still living at home. He reached for one of the boxes. He set a pan of water on to boil. Just then, he heard an announcement on the television, which made him rush back into the living room.

"We interrupt this broadcast for a special announcement from the President of the United States," sounded out the familiar voice of the local evening news reporter. The TV went black for a brief fraction of a second followed by a view of the President sitting behind his desk in the Oval office. He seemed more cheerful than usual. He held several papers in his hands and patiently waited for the cue from the camera personnel.

"Today we have achieved a major goal." He paused for effect then continued. "Inspired by former President Ronald Reagan we began the Strategic Defense Initiative Program. I am happy to announce that we have today achieved the goal of lessening the threat of global nuclear war." The President stopped as the photographers snapped pictures. He was in his element and loved the positive side of the news media coverage. "Earlier this week we successfully launched a total of nine defensive LBS satellites. As I speak, they are positioning themselves in geocentric orbit." A rash of snap shots sounded out as sporadic flashes of light temporarily blinded the President's eyes. Again paused until the press settled down and the room quieted. He looked over at his aids that reassured him with expressions that told him he was doing a fine job. With their confidence, he was sure he could win another term in office. And this announcement timed precisely in the middle of October would give him the Presidential image he needed to assure the defeat of the other party's snake in the grass candidate. Delaying this chain of events any longer was deemed unwise by his top aids. This would be a coup de grace over his opponent his cabinet assured him. Screw the opposition, they said, this is an election year.

"I repeat they are defensive satellites and are only a threat to intercontinental ballistic missiles. They are not a threat to any one singled out nation. I along with certain members of congress believe that by deploying this defensive system, we have assured ourselves of a world free of unchecked nuclear aggression." He had written the last part by himself and was particularly pleased. He thought it would assure his position in history as the President who brought ballistic peace to the world. No President since Reagan or Roosevelt would have more popularity at the poles than he would come November. He could smell victory already. The room became overwhelmed with applause and by the clicking noise of cameras. Someone yelled out:

"How will this effect our conventional forces stationed in Europe?" He was busting with pride and couldn't help but ad-lib. "Since my first term in office we have returned the majority of our standing armed forces to our own soil. Because of modern technology, we can send a conventional force anywhere in the world in less than twenty-four hours. The conservation of our military resources has greatly reduced our country's military budget and has been looked upon with admiration by fellow world powers." he smiled and looked over at his aids. They looked concerned, but still clapped their hands in time with the rest of the crowd. The President got the hint and went back to the written dialogue. This was no time for a slip up, but God, did he feel good! "Soon this defensive technology will be given freely to any nation which desires it. We, the United States of America, plan on deploying a total of 212 defensive satellites in all, but we believe that if other nations were to join us and send up their own, then out of this venture a truly united nation defense network can evolve. Such a defense league could insure that as mankind expands his activities out in space that military conquests would remain isolated events on our own planet. A future of a free and peaceful exploration of space would dominate. I reaffirm the United States of America can not, and will not, determine the political nature of other sovereign nations, but we must insure that political folly of a few does not lead to nuclear war and mass destruction on a nuclear scale. I believe that the deployment of this defensive system will meet our goals. And ... Now then, Members of the press, I know you have some questions for me?"

Paul went over and turned off the TV. He couldn't stand listening to the reporters ask their, in his opinion, inane questions. Of course it would effect the US / Russian /Chinese relations he thought to himself in response to the first question just before the screen went dark. He then went back to the kitchen, stood by the sliding glass door and looked out at the backyard. The garden needed to be weeded badly. He chuckled to himself then thought about it. Here it was, a world poised for nuclear destruction by countless Governments and terrorist groups, and he was worried about the condition of his garden. Weeds were insignificant compared to radioactive vegetables. The brief reprieve gave him a chance to collect his thoughts. He didn't know which was worse, being part of SDI, or not being informed on the current status of deployment. Moving dates up and rushing to get things done only increased the odds of failure. It also reflected on the instability on the part of the current administration. He had been led to believe the eventual deployment of the LBS's would be slow and cautious. This rash announcement stating they were already up there and that was that, was like storming into a hospital and yelling that the fire was under control. You might be able to calm some of the people, but you'll more than likely scare the hell out of the vast majority. Then again he thought, once up there, there is little anyone can do to bring them down. So maybe in the long run this was the best way to handle the situation. He didn't really believe this, but he had to come up with some reason to maintain faith in his government. If only they hadn't painted the picture to the general public that the satellites were purely defensive. This was more than a little white lie. A laser battle station could be called a protective shield on the one hand, but it could work just as well as an offensive lance. Only the programming alone decided the role it played. In the final analysis the government could do what it wanted and he could still feel relatively good about his participation in Star Wars. And if he didn't like the way things were turning out, he still had an ace up his sleeve. Studying Tim's tapes had given him a clue as to what he must do. He only hoped that he wouldn't have to implement his plan. In any event, he was ready.

"Jesus," he said out loud as he further pondered the ramifications. He promised his sons, through Helen that is, to keep them updated on how things were progressing. This revelation by the President would seriously undermine their trust. For all they knew, he was keeping this from them on purpose, that he had been one of the mainstream radicals all this time, and that he just pretended to be a skeptic in order to secure grandparent-visiting privileges. He quickly reached for the phone and dialed, but before it rang twice, he hung up the receiver. In case the line was tapped, he wanted to appear as a hard line hawk in favor of the Presidents decision at least a little longer. He turned back on the TV and changed the channel to the local all news station. There the speech was repeated along with the commentaries on its implications. A brief history of the SDI program was in progress when he received his first phone call from a reporter. The man wanted to ask him a few questions and Paul hung up on him. He wondered how he got his private number. A picture of the ever-pompous General Moorehouse flashed across the screen followed by a photo of him. The topic was people behind the project. His head pained him with the aspect of the publicity. The phone rang again. He hung up on the reporter who was rambling on and decided to get out of the house. He left a note for his wife to visit her mother for a few days while he went away to avoid the press. They were headhunters when a story was hot. He decided his wife would figure out that he went to Monterey. There he would stay in a small motel overlooking the ocean: the one that they had used so many times in the past. Looking out from the balcony at the kelp floating on the oceans surface, he could clear his thoughts and take a renewed perspective at the recent chain of events. Right now he was just too mad and frustrated. It wasn't the first time he had been left in the dark, just the most critical time. Just last week hi5 request to review certain segments of the ratified program was denied. He had argued that how could he uphold the quality control level required for such a program if he couldn't review its entirety whenever he wished? They flatly refused his request. They felt too much information in the hands of one man could have deleterious consequences. Basically after the disappearance of Timothy Winters, no one was kept in absolute trust. It was an intolerable situation. But knowing what little he did know, gave him distrust for the company and its intentions. The only reason for that frequency Clause was to give the US a first strike capability. For a country that professed the SDI system as solely defense oriented, this exception didn't fit well. He had to mentally sort things out. Helen could join him if she wanted.

He gathered his clothes in a small bag and dashed out of the house. The night before, he had parked on the street. While getting into the car he glanced up at the sky. The dark clouds looked ominous. Was it an omen or just a coincidence? He disregarded the view and pulled away from the curb. The surge of the car's power felt good.

CHAPTER 20

Paul could sense that someone was watching him when he left his house. He couldn't explain the feeling. He just felt uneasy. More like the self-conscious feeling you get when you knock over the stack of pickle jars at the neighborhood grocery store. You know everyone saw you do it, and you know they know you by name, but you still try to act as if someone else must have created the mess. Maybe he could explain the feeling after all.

As he got in the car and revved up the engine he expected someone to approach him. There was no one in sight. He backed out of the driveway, shifted into first, and screeched down the street. Nothing cleared his mind like driving fast. A few minutes down the road he saw the familiar sign of the local twenty-four hour convenience store called Jerry's Quick Stop. He pulled in and turned off the motor. He waited a moment, and then got out of the car. No one appeared to be following him. He stopped at this store many times in the past; he remembered the smell of Asian food that permeated the premises.

Inside the store he wandered over to the beer case and selected a six-pack of Coors. If he was going to go to the coast, then he might as well enjoy it he thought. He took the cold cans of beer over to the counter. A Pakistani gentleman wearing well-worn clothes and having a protruding stomach wore a pin on his shirt proclaiming himself as, Jake Sharee, store manager. He had begun began ringing up the beer on the cash register even before Paul reached the counter.

"I'll take two lottery tickets," Paul announced. He quickly spied a rack of Playboy's behind the counter. "Throw in a Playboy too." He hadn't read a fresh unwrinkled copy since his sons gave up Marvel Comics and he gave up his Playboy subscription just before his sons went away to college. The women that graced the pages were just looking too young. Jake turned and reached for the magazine. He added it all up.

"With tax, twelve seventy two." Paul gave him a twenty. All this time he kept a close watch on the parking lot. Nothing suspicious pulled into the lot. A couple of teenagers in an old beat up gas-guzzler sat outside, but God only knew what they were doing. A Pipe repair truck sat three spaces from the front door. The truck had been parked there before Paul arrived. The occupant looked as though he was ravenously attacking a ham sandwich and washing it down with a cup filled with Dr. Pepper. The beverage cup appeared bigger than the man's head. It wasn't until he left the store that he finally spotted what he thought had been with him all along. It was the lack of other nearby vehicles that attracted his attention to the car, and driver sitting inside it. A white car that looked like a BMW parked a short distant down the street. No it wasn't a BMW, it had the semi-v front silver grill of a Mercedes with the circular logo on the top of the hood. He thought it might be a 300 E, but couldn't be sure at this distance. His suspicions may have been over blown, but he couldn't help it. He tried to act as if he didn't notice the car, and placed the sack of beer and magazine behind the driver's seat of his Porsche. He stood with the door open and using his car key began to scratch off the silver substance on top of the lottery tickets that he had kept in his hand. He tried to glance over at the license plate as he rubbed of the spots, but the car was simply too far away to make out the letters or was it because he really needed to make that eye examination appointment like Helen suggested? He rubbed one card's surface completely clear off the silver substance that covered the numbers. He needed three matching amounts to win. The nine numbers were all different. He won nothing. He proceeded to slowly rub off the other card. Again he won nothing, but he smiled and acted as if he had won a couple of dollars. He shut the door to the Porsche and with the loosing tickets in hand, marched proudly back inside the store.

The man in the car took note of his actions, but found the movements unworthy of suspicion. Americans were a crazy people he thought. Separate the poor from the rich, but keep the poor pacified by giving them a one in a million chance to become rich. He personally preferred Russia's old system of fairness and equality. One didn't need to worry about being left homeless. The government took care of you. In fact, they did all the thinking for you too. There were too many choices in America: too many chances to go starving and homeless. Back home life used to be simple, uncomplicated, and all were treated equal. Although, he did have to admit that some were treated more equal than others; but what did he care. He could spend his working life in decadent America. He planned to retire back home, a privileged hand of the Party, but now, the party was over and he didn't know what to expect. He squeezed the steering wheel hard. His white knuckles exemplified his frustration with recent events.

The store was vacant except for the manager and several small boys huddled around the video machines.

"Do you have a phone?" Paul asked as he walked up to the counter. Jake raised an eyebrow and acted as if he had spoken to in a foreign language.

"You just passed the pay phone outside." He pointed out the window with his thick stubby fingers. Paul already anticipated his response. The pay phones were indeed outside and in direct line-of-sight of the car down the street.

"I'll give you five dollars if you let me use the one behind the counter. It's a local call," he quickly added.

"Where's your money." Jake shrugged his shoulders then set the old black dial-phone on top of the counter. His hand remained firmly gripped on it. Paul set a five-dollar bill next to the beat up looking phone. Fast as Paul could reach for the receiver, the money was pocketed and Jake moved off to straighten some papers on the far end of the counter.

"Operator, get me the police," Jake heard him say. Jake's dark brown eyes widened in surprise. What had he done? He only ate the sandwiches they could not sell. Surely they would not arrest him for that? Paul sensed the store clerk's apprehension. He waved his right hand; a half-assed don't worry gesture. Jake relaxed somewhat, but still looked puzzled.

"Yes. I'm at Jerry's Quick Stop on Blossom Hill Road. On the southbound curbside is a white 300E Mercedes. The man sitting inside has been waving a gun at pedestrians. It looks like a sawed-off shotgun. I'm calling anonymous. I think you better check it out." He hung up before he could be questioned. Jake said nothing, his shocked white, tabloid expression, said it all.

"That guy out there looks like a nut, and I didn't want to take any chances." Paul said just to make it sound more convincing. Jake appeared to understand.

"Here's your five back."

"What for?' Paul asked. He took it back anyway, and put it in his pocket.

"We don't need nuts around here. I see enough of them as it is." Jake folded his arms, shook his head, and leaned back against the counter. The position made his stomach swell out even more than usual. Jake made a good living he thought, but wondered how safe his job really was? Managers of small stores got shot in the face all the time, he knew it, he read it in the tabloids!

"We all have to do our part," Paul said feeling the camaraderie. Jake could tell he was lingering. He didn't blame him, but he couldn't think of anything to say. He kept one eye on Paul trying to figure him out, while keeping the other eye peeled for signs of the man with the shotgun.

"Can I get two more lottery tickets," Paul finally broke the silence. Jake bounced back to life. Another sale; he went into an automatic mode. He handed over the tickets and took the same five-dollar bill without saying a word or looking at Paul.

"Thanks," he didn't wait for Jake to return the change. He walked out of the store.

Standing beside his car, he began to slowly and meticulously rub off the silver strips. The car was still there. This time he won two dollars, but he was not about to re-enter the store. He began rubbing off the spaces on the other card and lost the game, but by then, a patrol car had pulled up in front of the Mercedes. The patrol car stopped some twenty feet ahead of the car, and then the officer began to radio in. Another unmarked car pulled up behind the Mercedes. The driver knew he had been out maneuvered. Even if he tried to leave now, the police would follow him. If he stayed, his subject would leave while he was detained with answering questions. His subject was a cleaver fellow. He most likely tipped them off, but he wasn't worried. It didn't matter what he told the police. His diplomatic immunity always made these encounters brief.

Paul watched as the police officer walked up to the car. His chest looked thick like he was wearing a bulletproof vest. It was his cue to get in the car and leave. He sped out of the parking lot. The patrol officer was concentrating on the job at hand and didn't hear Paul's tires screech with life. Feeling confident that his tail had been shaken, he headed straight for the coast. It was so much easier to outwit them, than beat them up the way they did in spy movies. He began to think about the westerns. It was the same scenario. In real life you shoot them in the back or ambush them. In the movies you have a duel at high noon; real life was never as dramatic, and a lot safer too.

He continued down the road wrapped up in his thoughts and didn't notice the other car following him from a safe distance. That is until he got to the Monterey coast turn off. He felt his chest sink in when he realized how naive he had been. He hit the accelerator and headed south on highway 17. They sensed he had spotted them and slowed down. Traffic was light however, so it was hard to blend in with other vacation bound vehicles. They tried to throw him off track, make him believe he was just paranoid, but Paul wasn't fooled for a moment. Two men in suits going down to the coast were just too obvious for a native Californian. Even the millionaires wore short-sleeved shirts around here. Paul kept his speed up until he entered a series of S-curves in the road halfway to Santa Cruse. He pulled over in a secluded spot at the first opportunity. He got out of his car and looked back down the road. The black BMW was just entering the first series of the curves. He ran back to his car. He had left the engine on and the door open. He reached behind the seat and grabbed the sack of beer. The cans were heavy and he thought the sack would rip, so he held it by the bottom of the sack. What he planned on doing was scaring off his would be tails. He knew they weren't FBI. After all, they had made themselves evident in the past, so it wouldn't make sense to change tactics now: that only left one agency as far as he was concerned, the KGB or its diehard remnants. He waited till the car emerged around the bend. It was going about forty. He gauged the distance and threw the sack containing his beer at the on coming car. He planned on sending it right through the open window on the passenger side and scarring the surprised occupants half to death. They might think it was a bomb or any number of things, but it would sure change the way they viewed their quarry. He had had it with them. Too bad there wasn't enough time to remove the Playboy. The bag sailed through the air as if in slow motion. He quickly determined that he hadn't allowed for the strong gusts of wind. The sack lurched upward and instead of landing in the passenger's lap, connected with the top edge of the front window. The windscreen crumbled under the weight of the projectile. Paul could hear the driver yell "Son of a bitch," in Russian. Although he didn't understand the words, the intonation made it perfectly clear. The driver swerved away from Paul and in the general direction of the cliff. Three hundred feet down was a sparsely forested valley. The driver immediately swerved in the opposite direction and ran off the other side of the road into a ditch and came to a stop at the bottom of a five-foot embankment.

"Jesus Christ." Paul said. He was scared spit less. He never expected this to happen. In fact he never expected anything really. He did it on impulse with little forethought. He wondered if he had killed them? No, he could see them moving in their car. He wondered if they would kill him? He dismissed the thought quickly. He ran to his car. He had to get out of here. He turned around and drove as fast as he dared. He couldn't believe what he had done. He had hit and run trained killers. He never thought himself capable of such madness. This scared him more than anything else he had ever done in his life! He would have felt better had he known the two men he had almost killed were the same one's that set fire to his former empire.

Dave and Carl saw something smash their windshield as they speeded around the bend in the road. Some type of high-powered shell shattered their windshield into a thousand pieces, but for some reason the majority of the window held in place. There was a three-inch diameter hole where the bullet must have entered inside their compartment.

"The Son of a bitch was armed I" Dave muttered as he regained consciousness. They expected to be fired at again at any moment, but they were both too sore to move. They heard a car rev up and leave. Dave got out of the lifted vehicle first. Something caught his eye. He walked over and picked up a can of beer lying on the ground. The can was cold. He pulled the tab and took a quick sip, and then he held the cold can against his aching head. Carl got out with some difficulty and looked at his partner in amazement.

"What the hell are you doing?" Dave didn't answer; he just picked up another beer and tossed it to Carl. Carl missed the catch, but never the less, reached down to pick it up. He found pulling the tab of the can back an excruciatingly painful procedure.

"The beer might help ease the pain." Dave found the Playboy half sticking out of a wet paper bag. He held it up and watched a golden colored liquid drain off.

"He killed Miss August," he sadly lamented.

"You're just as crazy as him. Let's get the hell out of here." Carl began limping up the embankment. Dave dropped the soggy magazine and dutifully followed with beer in tow.

CHAPTER 21

The sharp sound of someone knocking on the door awoke Paul. The motel room was pitch black, but he managed to find his way in the room. Half asleep he opened the door and peered out. The hall was empty except for the faint smell of the dead fish and dead kelp. He stood still for a moment and collected what little thoughts he had while trying to wake up. At first he wasn't even sure where he was, but the distant sound of the rolling waves finally caught his attention. Shaking his head, he glanced down at the newspaper conveniently placed by his feet. It didn't occur to him, that his was the only room that received a morning newspaper. It took most of his mental faculties just to become aware of the fact that he was standing stark naked in an open doorway.

Modesty gave him a shot of adrenaline and he quickly scooped up the paper, made a futile attempt to cover him with it, and shut the door. Back in the security of his darkened room he groped for a light switch. Rubbing the walls with his hands, he came across the bathroom light switch. No, the room's overhead fan turned on. He moved his hand around until his fingers came into contact with another switch. With a flick of an unconscious finger, light pored out of the bathroom. He turned the fan back off. Now, aided by the dim light, he headed back towards his bed. The idea was to throw the paper on the nightstand and go back to sleep. His sleep had been restless, and he felt the need for a few more hours in bed. In the process of trying to set down the paper, he clumsily knocked his watch along with several other items off onto the floor. He went through the motions of retrieving the fallen objects. This time he deftly set the newspaper on the stand, only to pick it up again as he glanced at the cover story. Unfolding it he held it close to his face and turned on the nightstand light. In big bold letters, the front page read, "WORLD CRISIS OVER SDI." The main article read as follows:

"US Says World Safe From ICBMS, Critics Argue US Holds Armed Fist Over Other Nations." The paper went on to report that a Chinese delegation team was expected to deliver a diplomatic communication to the President within 24 hours. The whole thing looked like a mockery of the Cuban missile crisis. What bothered him the most was that the entire front page was pro-star wars. Columns of articles praising the President for his courageous and aggressive stance in the name of ultimate peace, and therefore he must get total and undivided support. It was only on the second page that the paper mentioned in a small article, that large forces of Russians and Chinese were starting to concentrate near their perspective borders. Most of the columns were devoted to articles that went on to say, "When it came to space, Russia and China didn't care about a weapon's free environment, only who controlled the weapons". The journalists must have been hand fed this garbage straight from some nostalgic nerd. It was all cold war rhetoric and completely out of phase with restructured Russia or the newly emerging China. This was no halcyon affair. He knew what the Russians must have been thinking. The US overnight made their offensive as well as defensive weapons obsolete. What was left of the old guard would finally have that boost they needed to get the new parliament rethinking Russia's role in world politics. It left them clearly with one simple sobering thought. The phrase, "Either use'em or lose'em," no longer had meaning. The US had officially neutralized ICBM'S. Russia was stripped of its international military clout. Now, its Republics could break away at an even faster rate. The rest of the world could safely ignore Russia, now a toothless bear. The warring republics would destroy themselves while trying to gain independence, and many millions of people would die. A nice hot shower suddenly sounded real swell; one with water preferably radioactive free.

The shower didn't help much. Paul quickly shaved; only cutting himself during the short strokes on his jaw line, and then got dressed. He looked into the mirror, only a few drops of blood trickled down to his collar. He made another mental note to exchange razor blades before his chin became skinless. He went down to the lobby to checkout. With all that had transpired, even the sea breeze surroundings were not enough to detour his thinking. He felt it would be better to keep this little spot in the world strictly associated with happier times. Behind the counter slouched a tall thin college student yawning with one hand and holding down an open textbook with the other. Each page of the book was marked up in yellow highlight. Every other sentence was highlighted. Either the kid was behind in studies or doomed with a sea of information. He saw Paul, quickly shut the book, and stood erect.

"I hope you had a nice stay," he said as he took the room key from Paul.

"Fine as usual,' he answered. "Except for the knock at the door this morning," he added as an after thought.

"Knock at the door?"

"When the newspaper was delivered.' Paul recognized the blank expression on the kid's face. He needed say no more. It was odd he thought. He had stayed in this motel over a dozen times over a dozen years and never before had he received a newspaper. Self-serve dehydrated coffee in the lobby was about the only thing they did provide, so the paper was a mystery. Paul took a quick look around the lobby and spotted a well-dressed man in the adjoining walk-in restaurant. He was drinking a cup of fresh brewed drip coffee. The bulk of his body was concealed behind a trellis of assorted silk flowers, but from where Paul was standing, he could make out that the man was wearing a light blue sports jacket. Not the normal attire to go beach combing in. His eyes were fixed on Paul. Paul tried to act as if he hadn't noticed him and turned his attention back to paying the bill. He then walked briskly out of the lobby. Its not that he was frightened or anything, he just had a bad feeling about the situation and wanted to avoid it. Of course he did! He ruined a car, not to mention almost killing two of their agents. There was bound to be reprisals. Then he thought, maybe they already had. Maybe they destroyed his car last night while he slept and they were just waiting here now to see his reactions when found the mangled piece of metal. That must be what they did. That's what he would have done!

On his way out to his car, he heard a voice call out behind him.

"Dr. Crellin? May I have a word with you?" Paul turned around to face him. The heavyset man ran up to him briskly, although he looked like he wasn't enjoying the exercise.

"Are you CIA, FBI, or KGB?" Paul asked coldly.

"None of the above," the man said and chuckled. "I'm a diplomat."

"Well, what do you want?' The man gestured towards a white Mercedes." Can we discuss it in my car? I'm afraid your cases been bugged." His accent was east coast, probably Brooklyn, but there was something else to it.

"Your Russian aren't you," he pointedly asked.

"I'm afraid I am, but that doesn't make me a gangster does it?" Paul liked his quick cynicism and walked towards the man's car. Meetings in dark alleys must be a thing of the past he thought to himself. The man noticed Paul's eyes gazing at his Mercedes and mistook it as a sign of capitalistic desire to obtain all within reach. Something they were beginning to practice at home only at a more fundamental level with such items as toilet paper and bread.

"Had we taken over all of Germany," he paused until the bewildered former professor gave him his undivided attention. "The company that so skillfully crafted this precise piece of machinery would have used the same piece of metal to produce a shoddy tractor. So you see even die hard Soviets can admit their mistakes and pit falls. Call it a sign of the times. Or the state of the former Soviet Union Paul thought. His host grinned widely then said: "Oh please get in, the door is unlocked."

"Your not afraid of getting it stolen? This is America." He got inside the car. The man ignored him. Paul had heard the propaganda the old unabashed USSR disseminated. Things like poor people turned thieves roamed every street corner in America. Now it was truer of Moscow than in the Watts section of Los Angeles.

"It must be nice to leave your windshield wipers on your car instead of having to hide them until it rains." The man got in, shut his door and turned to Paul.

"Are you kidding? Only Russia's Mafia would waste its time stealing windshield wipers. Here, the thieves just take the whole car. The key was already in the ignition; he turned the radio on low. It probably never occurred to him that things weren't any better in the United States Paul reasoned. The man just thought his agents were responsible for keeping the capitalist pitfalls away from him. He was a walking dictum of die-hard soviet dialectical teachings; a recently reemerging antique gemstone of his motherland. It was another insight that KGB philosophy and ideology had not deterred the pace of reformation so desperately desired by the Russian middle class.

"What's going to happen to me?"

"No harm will come to you Doctor Crellin. These are all just precautionary measures. And yes the FBI thinks they are protecting you, but we have them following one of our own countrymen who could, and does, pass as your double." it sounded like something Dr. Frankenstein would tell his patients before surgery. 'Don't worry, we have more just like you.'

"And this is suppose to make me feel better?' Paul asked. The man looked surprised. He was used to people taking things at face value. Americans questioned everything. It was a wonder they ever got anything accomplished.

"It demonstrates that if we wanted to abduct you, we would have already done so. Therefore you can now be assured that what I'm about to say is sincere." He looked Paul eye to eye to appear more emphatic, and then a sullen mood overtook him. Paul could sense the gravity of what he was about to hear. "We know that your country has reserved a frequency, or a combination of frequencies, in order to secure a bypass on the SDI satellites program so you can initiate a first strike on Eastern Europe." Paul was not too surprised by this accusation due to Tim's involvement, but he wondered just how much information their espionage had accumulated.

"I could ask you for that frequency, but that would only prolong the problem. Sooner or later your country would find out we knew the frequency, forcing you to change it, then this whole episode would repeat itself." He leaned over towards Paul until he could sense that the American was uncomfortable. Staring into his eyes he said, "We are tired of playing games of life and death that neither of us can afford. We believe there may be another solution to the problem. One where all sides would be satisfied. We believe that you are one of the few men whose solution would be acceptable by all sides."

"My solution?" Paul interrupted.

"I might add that there are those outside of Moscow who would like to initiate a limited nuclear war. A test, shall we say, for you LBS system? They feel that they would find fault in its operation before its truly perfected."

"That's suicide," Paul snapped at him. "It is perfected!"

"I say this only to let you know how it has affected the rational of a prominent few." He paused for a second deep in thought. "Ugh, that is to say, those losing power anyway have little left to fear." It sounded like something Paul had read on a cereal box only worse.

"Stop the drama and tell me what is it you want me to do."

"Split them apart. Separate them so they don't all concentrate over, what was, the Soviet Union and China. Last but not least, make those satellites answerable to no single country."

"I could do the programming. It would take a couple of months to sort out, but that's not the problem."

"What is the problem?"

"In order to commit this treasonous act I would have to simultaneously gain direct access with each Battle Star, which can only be done through mission control in Houston."

"Then we will have to create a situation. One that will give them little alternative."

"You already have something in mind don't you?" Paul pointedly asked. These agents never missed a twisted trick.

"Oh, this is where your friend Mr. Winters will come in handy." Paul's eyes widened and he looked at him incredulously.

"Is he alive?"

"Oh yes. We have him in a rehabilitation station outside Novoi Sibiersk. The drugs took a toll on him, but he is doing better." An addict was just as good there as he was here, Paul guessed. Besides, there was little he could do. The subject quickly came to a close.

"So you see, we already have a good idea what to do. We just needed to see where you stood."

"You still have no guarantee that I'll cooperate," he protested. The man shook his balding head.

"You'll have little choice. Certain events will pass during the next few days. If you fail to do your part, then certain Generals will get their way. Remember that even one percent of our missiles launched would have devastating effects. And to be frank, we don't have the control over our weapons like we used to. Our society is dangerously fragmented." He paused for a moment. "Well, that's what I had to say, hope to see you again in the future."

Paul stepped out of the car without saying a word. What would they really do? He knew they had developed ground lasers to shoot down weather satellites, but LBS's were impervious to such obsolete tactics. So what could they do? They could try detonating nuclear devices in earth's upper atmosphere and create electromagnetic impulse waves. The generated pulses would ruin all electronic equipment in orbit long before the LBS's succumbed to such a force. They were built with this factor in mind. Thermonuclear fall out wouldn't be a problem either, but the act itself might lead to global warfare. Not a very good outcome, with peace breaking out around the world, and only possible if the nuclear devices could explode close enough to the LBS's in the first place. The entire episode could have been one of the best bluffs the East Europe hard-liners had ever come up with. On the other hand, the sincerity of this man was overwhelming. Maybe some vanquished former-soviet officials were ready to retaliate with nuclear war. Limited or whole scale war wouldn't much matter. Both sides would be overcome by the thought of using every last missile. Worse, the system until used was pure theory. Even the best experts could be wrong on the percentages. What a God Damn intolerable situation he was in. Then he thought for a moment, he smiled, he got an idea. It was simple; he would prepare himself for both sides. What could he lose? By the end of the week he would either be known as a traitor to his country or the man who could have stopped Armageddon. Well, maybe not anything that sounded so heroic, but at least he could get mention on page three as the man who helped resolve an inconvenient situation. Besides, the choice was simple. He had to believe in his country. He had to believe that a few military diehards were just out to confuse his ideology and loyalties. They were the enemy, not all of them of course, just a few leaders that clung to tried and failed out of favor beliefs. They were waiting for a chance to regain political and military control; Paul would be ready just in case.

Chapter 22

Monday morning Paul arrived at Wescon Industries with no idea what to expect: a debriefing by the FBI for having spoken to a foreign diplomat, an entourage of reporters all wanting an exclusive byline on the anti-ballistic missile system? But what he got instead was a grueling office meeting and a congratulatory speech by General Moorehouse himself. The General was well aware of Paul's discontent for being kept in the dark on the launching dates. Just before the meeting, he took Paul aside and reasoned with him that it was imperative to let as few people know as possible. He also knew Paul considered the project his own pet and therefore he would be more emotionally impacted by the issue than really necessary. Still, he hoped Paul would understand. He would have to understand. A few days to relax before his next project would do him a world of good Moorehouse reasoned. The SDI project no longer concerned him; the program would require little if any maintenance.

Paul went home after the meeting and secluded himself from all household events and returned to working on the various scenarios. A major endeavor for just one man, and there was not much time left. To add to his difficulties, his thoughts were distracted by his ever-present conscience. If what he was attempting was unveiled as espionage, it could cost him a life in prison. The trick therefore would be to have his plans ready to use or loose as fast as possible. His work on the SDI program officially completed, any further work could be used as evidence against him. He would now straddle a fine red line.

The task at hand seemed insurmountable and the evening's work did not progress very far. To keep from having a night of insomnia he took two of his wife's sleeping pills. The effects were more than he bargained for. He fell fast asleep fast. Hours later found himself, head under a pillow looking at the clock. The time read twelve o'clock. The light coming from the window confirmed the time as noon.

"I thought you would never wake up," Helen said. Paul rubbed his eyes then opened them to find a cup of coffee with cream held out in front of him.

"Thanks honey." He raised himself to a sitting position in bed and took the mug from her hand. The coffee smelled strong and refreshing. Not the way Helen normally brewed it, but the way he liked best.

I've been worried about you lately," she continued. "I know we haven't spent much time together the last couple of months and I was hoping that now that your finished with those satellites, we can take a vacation. Just the two of us.'" He looked at Helen as if she had made a cosmic revelation. She hadn't talked like this since he started his own company. He never realized how depressed she had become after the fire. She concealed it well, but her aspirations for the family had since fallen to the side.

"That sounds nice, but the project might take a little longer than expected." He had to stall for time. He wanted to go with her, but this was the worst possible moment; if not the most critical.

"I'm fed up with your project," she shouted out. She sat on the bed and rubbed her forehead. "I feel like your dating another woman. You don't even look at me anymore. You just drift off and stare at the walls. You mumble strange things in your sleep. Its worse than when you first lost the business." She didn't mean to say it like that, but she was exasperated. It wasn't the first time she thought about how distant their lives had grown apart. She tried to think about what they still had in common, but came up empty handed.

He looked at her round figure. Sure she had gained a little with age, but her breasts were still firm and her wrinkles were hardly noticeable. He stared at her figure in a way he hadn't done for a long time. Then he looked into her eyes. Those eyes that had once captivated him in his youth still penetrated and stirred deep buried emotions. It saddened him that things had upset her so.

"I'm sorry," he said regretfully. "But if you want I'll quit as soon as I've completed this last assignment."

"I don't want you to quit. That would be like sending you to prison. I'm just tired of being a wife without a husband." He stretched, got out of bed, and reached for his robe.

"I think I'll take a shower." He wrapped the robe around himself. "We can talk more over lunch."

"It can't wait," she said with a sigh. His eyes widened as he saw the over-night bag lying beside her feet. It was stuffed full.

"Where are you going?" he asked half anticipating what the answer would be.

He knew the relationship was on edge, which had been plain well before the sons left home.

"I'm going to visit the boys. I think one of us should stay in touch with them." He knew this phrase verbatim. She said it in spite of herself. She knew perfectly well why they didn't want to see their father. That was their problem, not his, yet he was faced with the blame.

"When will you be back"?

"When you're finished with your work and ready to take some time off. She then pressed her lips firmly together to keep from crying, picked up her bag, and left the bedroom. Paul wavered for a moment, then hopped in the shower. The warm water felt good on his fatigued body. On purpose he plunged his face under the flow of pulsating liquid. He tried to erase from his mind the scene that just transpired. There were more important things to deal with than a marriage falling apart years ago. Especially when the rest of the world was falling apart even faster. Or was he just thinking this way to clear his mind for the other problem at hand?

The ringing of the phone broke his serenity. Damn, he thought to himself. He pictured himself twisting the phone apart. He was damned if he was going to answer it. In fact, he decided he wouldn't answer it the rest of the day. He wanted no interruptions. Already he compiled a crude program that could possibly be amended to the main program, but ft needed a strict concentrated review to make sure ft wasn't a worthless piece of garbage. Inherent faults could abound. The speculations and questions were endless. More often than not, even the mere incision of a single binary dot could wreck havoc on the main program, and here he was adding several hundred lines composed of thousands of binary signals. To make his insert version less than crude, it would require thousands of lines. But all those lines would require too much time to word them right, so he was forced to devise something short and simple.

Only in a few instances did he rely on his subprogram to interact with portions of the main program. He surprised himself with how fast he put the subprogram together.

Working solely on the main program for the last two years made the task possible. Few other people could have done it at all, let alone within the allotted space of time. This wasn't anything he would brag about, it's just that not many people were privy to the necessary background information. Feeling confident with what he accomplished during the long night, he went about his morning rituals in a leisurely fashion. No electric shavers today. He took his time. In his opinion warm lather and a sharp blade gave a closer, smoother, shave, but who had time for it?

Paul dressed and went into the kitchen. The house was extra quiet. He thought he saw the shadow of something through the kitchen window. He looked closer and saw nothing. 'I'm losing my mind," he said to himself. Visions of spy versus spy climbing all over his house were not those of a sane man. The world was just too quiet.

The light was still illuminated on the coffee maker. Drinking coffee in bed was rather unusual and he had forgotten about the half filled cup setting on his nightstand.

Damned, they were doing all right. If only she knew the importance of his work, then she'd understand. Yet, she never did in the past he reflected. It had been the same way when he had first started out in the field. She never understood him completely; still, their marriage had remained cohesive all these years. What was it that drew them together? When his business initially collapsed, she spent some soul-searching time at her mother's house. Because of her mother's recent death, she now stayed with the children. Damn. Why was it that he always thought more about her when she was gone than when she was near?

Paul took another cup out of the cupboard and filled it to the brim. A few drops spilled over the side and landed on the floor. Out of reflex he looked around, relaxed a little, then took a sip. The floor could wait until just before she returned. He knew she hated a dirty house and their was enough tension already between them. He made a mental note to retrieve the cup from the bedroom sometime later on in the day. As usual he forgot about it in the same breath and the contents would dehydrate into dust before the issue came up again. If Einstein had been as poor at remembering things as he was, relativity might never have arrived in this century. He took another sip and grimaced.

The coffee had been boiling down to a hotter stronger potion than he was used to. He drank enough to make some room, and then added a little cream to the elixir. With cup in hand, he went to his study.

"Jesus!" He blurted out as he looked at his screen. He had finished up late the previous night and he must have been more fired than he thought possible. He checked the screen again. His eyes strained in disbelief. Within the first hundred lines of the program he had worked so hard on, he found several major flaws. This wasn't like him. It must be the pressure. The idea of being manipulated by the Russians must have been too much. Without proper authorization, the implementation of his handicraft would rate more than treasonous. They wanted the LBS's to be useless security ornaments in the sky. Maybe that was it. Maybe his subconscious was trying to tell him something he couldn't bring himself to believe. The Russians could care less what happened to him. So what if he did what they demanded? Who would believe him? 'I had to do it'. He could hear himself telling the Senate. 'Otherwise a few Russian extremists threatened to destroy the world.' He would be lucky if all they gave him was, a padded cell. Maybe he was cracking up. That would explain the overlooked mistakes on his program. That would explain the recent round with his wife. It would explain a lot of things. Then he thought for a moment; the meeting with the agent came back to mind. He said they had Tim in custody. If his condition remained stable, there was no telling what they could coerce him into doing. Holding drugs in front of him they could lead him around in any direction. Using Tim, they could sabotage the entire program.

Then again, if that was their goal, they didn't need Paul's help. Which led him to believe that their offer was genuine. Sure there may have been a few officials that wanted to use Tim for unscrupulous reasons, but the overriding priority in the Russian hierarchy would be to secure a non-dominating defense network. Even the US authorities would have to concur with this logical conclusion. However, even in the US, one couldn't rule out whether the government would react with ideological consistency.

So where did that leave him? Right back where he started. He would abide by their wishes, which he felt had no deleterious consequences for his native land. This could possibly lead him down the road to wearing a white wrap around leather jacket inside a nicely padded white cell; the chances of this occurring seemed to be about fifty/fifty, which was a gray area he could currently deal with.

CHAPTER 23

General James Moorehouse stormed into the briefing room.
Sitting around an elongated black veneer table, eighteen assorted
officers and scientists held gloomy expressions on their faces. The
General glared at no one in particular as he made his way to the far
end of the table. Wednesday morning, he thought. Only the
middle of the week and already all Hell had broken loose. His
main contractors at the pentagon were ready to shit bricks and he
didn't even advise them as to how bad things really were. Heads
were going to role and he was damned if his head would wind up
on some silver platter. His assistants were useless he reconciled.
The two assistants did their best to keep up with his pace.
Weighted down with over-stuffed briefcases made the task more
difficult. They knew the General well, and they both were
sweating profusely. Moorehouse was a man with a low tolerance
level. If he got mad, that was it. It was all out war after that, and
that was precisely the reason he had to relinquish his command in
the military: too many needless incursions, too many homebound
body bags for his superiors to be able to rationalize.

"Now then, I want to hear it as if I've never heard it before
and don't leave out any details." He tried not to scold them too
much for he realized scientists were a touchy bunch, but inside he
was furious. He sat down in a large cushioned black leather chair,
folded his arms, and wafted patiently, like a mother waiting for her
sons to confess their crimes. A brief second passed then one of the
scientists spoke up. It was Patrick Chandler, one of Wescon's SDI
sub-program directors and a true Bostonian that graduated from
MIT. Moorehouse's attitude ticked him off, but he was determined
not to stoop to the General's level. He started out soft and
monotonous.

"As you were already informed, a modified version of a
Soviet built SS24 missile was accidentally launched in northern

Uzbekistan. Their not part of the new Russian federation, by the way. The Russians called the President immediately. They made a formal apology and asked if we would destroy the missile in flight. They gave us its trajectory and said that the safety device failed to detonate. That's all they could do at their end." He took a deep breath, gestured with his hands held out. "They basically dumped it in our lap."

"So we had an uncontrollable missile," Moorehouse quickly snapped, trying to pick up the pace of the story. Leave it to a scientist to make something as exciting as this sound like the summer weather report in Hawaii; which never changed and was as boring as hell to listen to. Patrick Chandler stopped as if to collect his thoughts, but he was using this time to annoy the General even further. The military mind, even if ex-military was just too reactive. If he didn't want to hear the whole story, then why didn't he just ask specifics?

"If I may continue, our Battle Stars should have destroyed the missile in the launch phase, but for some inexplicable reason, didn't. We don't know why. We are working on that right now. But this isn't the worst of it." He sighed in disappointment.

"The SS24 in question for no apparent reason self-detonated prior to re-entry into the atmosphere. We can't rule out that it was deliberately planned. One of our LBS stations took the brunt of the after shocks. And although the ensuing explosion was not as great as expected, we still don't know what the net effect will be. Our guesstimations don't look promising. We do know however, that LBS number one, five, and six, have all turned themselves on to full alert." He stopped and looked straight at the General. Moorehouse slumped in his seat a little, or was he just bracing himself. His hand waved in gesture for Patrick to continue. He knew Chandler always saved the worst for last.

"Some how, the LBS's that is, have bypassed DEFCON 2, defense condition two, and went directly to DEFCON 1, which for those of you who haven't dusted off your manuals lately, is the state of war. Again there is no explanation, we don't know, but we are working on it." This time the pausing to reorganize his thoughts was real. He didn't like being the one without the answers. The expression, 'I don't know', had bugged him since his childhood. Now he found himself forced to repeatedly say it to a man also becoming infuriated with the use of that phrase; and still the worst was yet to come. With another deep breath he continued. "This brings us to the current situation. LBS five has changed orbit in response to these events. Just a few minutes ago we calculated that within the hour it will be in the near vicinity of a Soviet Sea Rescue Satellite. If it truly is on full alert, then we might as well say it's on a collision course. It will probably attack anything in close proximity that's bigger than a pickle. Real soon the President will have to explain the LBS's defensive capabilities over the hot line to the Russians and why they no longer have an orbiting SEA rescue satellite. And that about wraps it up." With the wipe of his handkerchief, he removed the forming beads of sweat from his forehead. The pressure was unbearable. It wasn't his fault, but as spokesperson, he did feel his full share of the responsibility.

"The President doesn't have to do anything!" Moorehouse's voice boomed out.

"Can we turn it off?"

"I'm afraid not," one of the other scientists spoke up. "Number five won't respond."

"What about the other two satellites? Are they going to stray too?"

"Were not sure," the same man responded. 'But a domino effect can't be ruled out." Patrick Chandler's voice trailed of to a soft whisper. General Moorehouse wondered if he was already calculating in his head what would happen next. The man was a genius. They were all top intellectuals by God. And look what they had gotten him into. The crisis first, then save your own bloody ass, later, he hurriedly said to himself.

"Any ideas how that SS24 went undetected by our SATS? That thing carries over twenty five thousand pounds of thrust. Something should have detected it!" He searched the faces in the room for anyone to speak up. His eyes caught the familiar eyes of a soldier and they settled on him.

"Major Hennessey sir." Moorehouse nodded at the colorful olive green uniform.

"Sir, intelligence has come up with a plausible reason why this has happened."

He wasn't used to telling anything but solid facts and the idea of repeating mere conjecture to the General seemed highly irregular, but everything was unconventional in a civilian atmosphere. With a parched throat he went on," We think a renegade faction of Ukrainians did this to deliberately disgrace both Russia and our SDI stratagem. There is substantial evidence that Mr. Winters, a former employee of Wescon, is being held somewhere in Eastern Europe. If he is, then it follows that he could have given them the necessary frequencies to get the SS24 off the ground. The frequencies were changed on a number of occasions, but that may not have stopped someone with his skill and abilities. This would also coincide with the just too accurate timing and position of the spontaneous detonation.

"If that's true, then why didn't they take the opportunity and blast them out of orbit? That missile could have detonated closer and done more damage. And why just one missile?"

"Too risky sir. This way they get other nations to focus their attention on us, and force us to bring the SATs back down through political means. Or they maybe trying to figure out a way to take control of them for their own motives." Moorehouse leaned back in his chair while rubbing his right fist against his chin. He never liked shaving with an electric shaver and his skin was itching like mad, or was it just nerves. He hadn't felt this way in years.

"Recommendations?" he ended the silence.

"First we prepare the President for the worst," one of the women in the group said. Susan Chan was with Army Intelligence, a Captain, but she wore no uniform to distinguish her rank. Even her laminated security badge looked like a civilian's. Moorehouse had known of her for seven years before he could prompt the boys in the Pentagon to put her on his staff. She was always worth listening to. She was straight forward and uncannily picked the best course of action to take. The rest of the room fell silent as the listened to each word. "Secondly, we find out if the problem with number five is mechanical, or in the program itself, and if so, is the problem going to crop up in the other SAT'S? And last, we find out if Mr. Winters has indeed fallen into the hands of some renegade holdouts. If he has, then we act accordingly." Coming from her, which could not rule out a convenient accident.

One could never take her lightly. Borderline psychopaths could never be taken lightly!

"Very well." General Moorehouse turned back to Patrick Chandler. 'How much time will it take to evaluate the programming end of this mess?'

"Hard to say General. Very few of us have seen the entire program let alone physically worked on it." That's not what the General wanted to here. He wanted optimism and he wanted it now!

"Where in the Hell is Dr. Crellin?"

"We haven't been able to reach him," another unsuspecting victim with a deep voice answered.

"Well go get him. Drag him in here. Whatever ft takes; send some men for him. I want him here two minutes ago. Got that?"

"Yes sir," a man saluted and left the room.

"Meeting adjourned." He rose out of his chair and marched out of the room confident that action was now underway. The others stood as he left, even the scientists. It was hard not to get swept up by the General's magnetism when he so desired. The crisis was still out of control, but at least the members were unified. The battle was half won, he thought as he strode with a military gate towards his office. Inside he would make the overdue call to the President. Damn, what a mess they were in.

CHAPTER 24

Hard at work on his sub-program he barely heard the knock on the front door. Instinctively his fingers pushed the copy button and by the time he had raised out of his chair, the copy was finished. He pulled out tape and turned off the machine. The doorbell began to ring repeatedly. Putting the tape in his shirt pocket, he went to greet the noisemaker.

"Dr. Crellin? We're here to escort you directly to Wesson Industries," a short well-built man wearing a dark blue company security uniform told him. He looked more like a Marine corp. serge than a security guard. As an after thought Paul wished this muscular figure had been working for him prior to the fire of his own corporation. Paul brought his attention back to what the man said. He had made ft sound like an order. Was this how he intended it to sound?

"You mind telling me why?"

"Sorry sir can't say. My orders are to bring you in to Wescon, ASAP."

"Ok, just give me a minute to get a jacket." It was warm outside, but the office was always too efficiently air-conditioned for his tastes.

"Ok sir." The stocky man entered and followed right behind him. Paul grabbed a sweater from the closet and the three of them got in a large black limousine. One drove while the stocky Bulldog sat in the back, directly across from Paul. His eyes never left him for a moment. He didn't have time to ditch the copy of the tape before leaving the house. The guard had been standing right behind him watching his every move. Now, he would have to carry the tape with him and pray he wasn't searched. He knew he was dead if they found it on him. He could see it now; iron bars and branded a traitor to his country. He wondered what the stocky man was thinking. Paul glanced at the man's hands. The fingers looked like they had been broken in many places on numerous occasions; the way a martial arts instructor's would resemble. This theory subdued Paul's mood. He had to be an agent from some branch of the law, but he wasn't giving information away. Suddenly he felt a horrid feeling. Maybe they were rogue KGB. When would he ever learn? He should have protested before leaving his house. They just looked too professional to argue with. He hadn't fired or been around a gun since his youth, but he could recognize the outline of a holster under the man's left arm. There was little reason to protest his abduction in order to see the caliber of their weapons; he decided it would behoove him to go with the flow instead.

For several minutes he gazed out the one-way tinted windows. Looking at nothing in particular. Across from him the man lowered one arm and opened a drawer previously hidden beneath the seat directly behind his aides. Paul examined the drawer's contents.

"Like a candy bar or some gum?" His host asked him. They were American all right.

"No thanks," he replied. "Do you have any music?"

"Turn on the radio," the man rasped as he knocked on a glass window that divided the driver from the rear occupants. The radio came on with light easy listening rock. It was fine, anything to break the silence. Another ten minutes passed then abruptly a female newscaster reported:

"The details from the Pentagon are still sketchy, but it appears that one of the Star Wars Satellites has malfunctioned and at 1:15 today attacked and destroyed a Russian Sea Rescue Satellite after having been attacked, itself, by a lone renegade former Soviet built SS24 missile. Sources say this is an isolated event and both governments are looking into the matter. The Russians have apologized for their former Republic of Uzbekistan's launching of the missile and claiming it was due to a malfunction in the arming mechanism. They claim that this missile was a prototype and that this event is highly unlikely to reoccur. We'll have more news and sports after these messages."

"I think your friend can switch it off now." The man tapped on the glass at about the same time the other driver turned it off.

The car was bugged inside out. What an ironic coincidence, he thought as he watched the scenery roll by. The diplomat told him there would be a sign. It seemed impossible. Still, the implications were grave. Had a faction of Russians found a crude, but effective, way to control them? Was there a mechanical malfunction leading to a runaway LBS or was it planned with precision? Or worse, a flaw in the software? The fact that he was being dragged in was ominous in itself. He sat in silence the rest of the trip.

"Here we are,' one of them spoke up as they passed the security check point at the front gate of Wescon Industries. Paul noticed the extra security guards on hand. They were nothing like Clarence Omalery, his former security guard; these men were fit and trim. They looked like they just came off of combat duty and were ready to strike again. He could have never afforded to hire such professionals for his own small private company.

The car pulled up to the entrance of the building and a security guard who he had never seen before, opened the car door. The bright burgundy colored granite walls of the building had been washed that morning and the steps were still wet. He got out of the car and carefully walked up the stairs. The man sifting across from him followed behind him while the driver sped away in the car. Through the thick glass doors of the building he was met by the smile of General Moorehouse. Apparently his henchmen had notified him of Paul's arrival.

"General." Paul nodded and went inside. He was apprehensive yet ecstatic that Moorehouse was in such a discomforting position. Never the less, the smile showed no signs of wavering.

"I'm glad we found you. Dr. Chandler is waiting in your office to fill you in on the details." Paul nodded his head again then passed by him. Moorehouse remained standing with his hands clasped in front. Obviously waiting patently for the cadres of government officials that would be descending in times like these. Paul proceeded to his office without another thought about the General and his associated political turmoil. In his office he found Patrick Chandler eyes glued to the desktop computer screen.

"Thank God your here!" Chandler began. He proceeded to give the details as to what had transpired so far. In final analysis

Paul's estimation of what the renegades had done was fairly accurate, and he was relieved that the situation had not been more serious. As they stood, things could be corrected with minimal effort. Of course he couldn't tell Chandler this. He had to play it out as long as possible. He needed time to weigh his options, his consequences, and a way to transmit the solution simultaneously to each individual battle station. Would the company and NASA give him a direct link to the LBS'S? He doubted it, but time was on his side, not theirs. Another day of unharnessed chariots of war in orbit and foreign relations would go down the tubes. The first thing then was to play the part of the fool while working on his own sub-program. He still was far from having it perfect. Then he could concentrate his efforts on the link up. It would probably be easier to make contact with aliens or have the government solve the foreign trade deficit, but he would try just the same.

He spent the majority of the afternoon trying to piece together a series of commands that would put the battle stars back in a more peaceful alert mode. The commands were easy enough, but without returning the LBS's to their prior orbits, there was no guarantee they would stay in any particular condition for very long. So far the signals had been patched through to Houston and then beamed up. They kept everything delayed as to note its progress and determine at both ends if all was in order. The process dragged on at a snail's pace. Paul worked on his own solutions during the off-line periods. He wondered what good it would do though, if they couldn't resolve the haunting question in the back of everyone's mind: If a clandestine group of radicals were behind all this, as suspected, then they knew something significant about the over-all program code that his side didn't. That left him at a severe disadvantage. The renegades had Timothy Winters, and he worked on this program three straight years before his disappearance. That's a hefty lead-time for someone with a mind like his. There's no telling what subtle nuances he previously inserted into the project's main program. With millions of lines of data, he could have created virtual chaos. He could be the king of computer viruses if he so desired. The present dilemma suggested however, that a more controllable purpose was in mind. Paul was now led to believe the Russians were sincere with their previous proposal. Hard to believe they could be sincere about anything in these strange times, but if they already balked at the idea of trying to utilize the killer SATs for their own perversions, then there was little left to doubt. They must fear LBS deployment more than they did the nuclear bombs when those hellish weapons first went public. The Russians, as well as the Chinese, are advanced in certain theoretical areas of LBS technology, but their physical progress has been slow. There so called bureaucracy only helped to slow them down even further. And because of their past, they were now too cash strapped to do anything but keep the Russian federation from dissolving into chaos. The dawn of the computer age had not even arrived for the average former-east block scientist. They were just too poor to own personal computers. They didn't need information; they needed foreign subsidies for buying food and basic housing goods.

Perhaps all this was just a small short-term problem. With the former-common wealth of independent states about to explode with over seventy million Muslims, pure Russians could find themselves a minority trying to fit in unobtrusively. They'd need all their resources to curtain border disputes within the existing unified states. The problem already began to boil over in places like Chechnya, Georgia, and the Ukraine. It was an issue already hamstringing the policies of those trying to retain political control. The accumulated effects could be devastating. The setbacks the Russians faced over the last few years had to have an accumulative and caustic effect on the nation's well being. SDI might not only be the straw that broke the bear's back, but caused it to join the ranks of extinct Mammoths that also once roamed across the Russian plains. Keeping this in mind, securing world peace would be a very noble last gesture by a nation ready to be known as only a footnote in world history. So many Russians had given their lives for their country; the US had to help them more now than ever, otherwise the amount of Russian bloodshed would only increase as Russia neared its final days.

"What have you got so far?" one of the General's aids bolted into the room and hurriedly asked. He appeared out of breath and seemed anxious for Paul to respond. Paul looked up from the screen, his eyes glaring at the young man in the white lab coat. Paul forgot his name, but he knew he was one of the new whiz kids. He had the talent. He just needed the experience before taking over Paul's job. There were half a dozen just like him employed by Wescon Industries.

"You just can't rush this." Paul said.

"The General wants an up date. We've determined that unless we do something soon, Battle Star three is headed on a collision course with Buran, the Russian space shuttle." He remembered the name; it was called Snowstorm in English. It had had several major setbacks in the past, but a year ago finally made it into orbit. The Russians were back in space.

"What the hell is that doing up there?"

"The Russians sent it up right after LBS number eight lifted off. We think they did it to monitor our SATS."

"Then its simple, they'll just have to move that piece of junk," Paul said matter of fact.

"Polite suggestions have failed, they either think they own God damn space or they want to test LBS capabilities. Publicly they've claimed an on board technical failure, so they can't return home yet, but we know this is bullshit."

"How long before lock on by number three?"

"Six more hours."

"That would put ft right around midnight. Are the Russians aware of this?"

"Not as to the exact time yet. We might be wrong ourselves." The whiz kid looked at the screen trying to change the topic. "So what have you got so far?"

"We've come up with a solution that might work, but I still don't know what the problem was in the first place. So what we have is only a good guess." The young assistants face lighted up with hope.

"That's good news. The General wants you to give me what you got and patch it over to the control room. They'll send it to Houston on the private channel."

"But its not ready," Paul insisted.

"That's an order," the aid shouted back at him. The sound of this had a NAZI Germany ring to it. Handing over his work meant loosing control of the program for his own purposes, but what could he do? He slammed his fingers against the keyboard and sent what he had over to the control room. There must be another way he thought optimistically.

"There all mad as March Hares," Patrick spoke up. He came into the room just after the aid left. He'd been in and out of Paul's office most of the day. "They want everything overnight and out of the hands of those that should be in control."

"How much you want to bet it won't work?" Paul asked him: his sarcasm plain by his tone of voice.

"What do you mean?" Chandler had a puzzled look on his face. "I helped you write it. It was good." Paul shrugged his shoulders.

"They want a quick cure, but I think the symptoms run a lot deeper. I think the only way were going to fix this problem is by having an open dialogue with the little bastard battle stars themselves. Something they don't want me or anyone else to do."

"So what are you going to do now?"

"I think I'll just lay back on the sofa and take a nap while they find out I'm right." He proceeded to stretch out on his tiny office couch and closed his eyes. Without looking, he pressed one foot against the other until both shoes came off and fell to the floor. Cocky son of a bitch, Chandler thought.

"Good night." Patrick Chandler shut the door and headed towards the control room. He couldn't believe how cool the man was taking this. It may not have been interesting for the famous Dr. Crellin because of his insight, but for him, this was living history. He couldn't waft to see the results of his co-created instructional program. He expected its impact to be tremendous.

CHAPTER 25

Lying on the sofa gave Paul time to sift through several possible solutions. Over and over he played with different scenarios in his mind. However, until he could gain direct access to the battle stars, there was no way he could alter their primary orbits, and he couldn't foresee any hope of gaining such access. The security personnel didn't trust many people and with good reason too. His thoughts were abruptly halted when Patrick Chandler burst into his office. The sudden noise startled Paul; he opened his eyes and rose to his feet. He felt off balance until the blood re-circulated to his head. Patrick began speaking, slightly out of breath.

"You won't believe what has happened. The President has just received a diplomatic communiqué from the Russian ambassador. No one else knows what it says, but the Strategic Command has been put on alert, and there are reports that large contingencies of Chinese forces are concentrating along the northeast section of the Russian/Chinese border. And there is talk of another military coup attempt in Moscow. They've been waiting for something like this to take back control of their country. The press is going wild. They've released a front-page mystery crisis report just like the ones during the Cuban missile crisis. Someone from the latest Russian government has released a statement saying that if any more mishaps occur due to the poorly designed Death Beacons, we call satellites, they would hold the US responsible. Imagine them saying that; after all, it was their SS24 missile in the first place that started all this." He took a second to catch his breath. Paul sat in silence as he thought about what would probably happen next. "Ah, they don't say they'll make a retaliatory strike, but the papers report the delegate said that such an act will be met by whatever actions were deemed necessary.

They must have anticipated all this and that's why they sent up Buran. They must have determined that with thousands of pounds of thrust our SATs would have destroyed it on lift off if they waded any longer." He walked over and sat in the chair next to Paul's deck. His breathing rate slowed a little, but his forehead still showed signs of heavy perspiration.

"I think your right," Paul stated. Patrick Chandler looked at Paul oddly. He hadn't expected Paul to take this so calmly. The world was failing apart and all this man could do was muster a one-line sentence of recognition.

"Of course they don't know how well our LBS's can distinguish ballistic missiles from other objects, so they must have been planning for a worst case scenario. Damned paranoid fools! They've probably got that thing armed with every useless device they could get their hands on." Paul casually stretched his arms as he listened. Patrick began to wonder if Paul had recently taken any sedatives.

"I take it that the batch file wouldn't work," he said it more like a statement than a question.

"Oh, we think it works, but we can't get those crazy space mines to accept our data." Paul knew, all too well, just how close to reality Patrick's phrase 'space mines' was.

"Any idea what the problem is?"

"The frequencies match up, and we can receive signals, but for some strange reason, we can't get the LBS's to receive anything.' Paul knew the implications all too well. It all pointed towards Timothy Winters. If that many people could sift through the main program and come up with nothing, then there had to be something imbedded between the lines. A sub-program, or batch file, neatly buried under mounds of data. The set of commands had to be developed by someone with a very special talent. The problem was, if it took Tim years to subtly infuse K, then it would take him at least that long to root it out. Not a very immediately promising prospect.

"Got any ideas," Patrick could visualize the wheels in Paul's mind spinning. He wished he had his accumulated background knowledge. Paul gave him an uncertain expression, as if he was ready to say yes, and then changed his mind.

"If I could gain direct access to the satellites, I might be able to figure out where the problem lies." Sure it might take a year he thought, but at least it was a step in the right direction.

"I anticipated your request and already approached the General on the subject." Paul's eyebrows lifted up.

"Oh, what did he say?" he could taste his triumph. Patrick proudly announced,

"They're waiting for you in the control room. Houston is patched through. They weren't too happy about it, but what choice do they have?"

"What are we waiting for?" Paul said as he pushed his way past him. It was hard to control his excitement. This kid is going places he thought.

Paul stood in the control room. A large room filled with technical instruments, computer consoles, white sterile walls, and fired looking faces. He was ecstatic. He finally had one on one control of the entire computer system of Wescon Industries. There were other control rooms across the country for Wescon was a giant in the computer industry, but this was the master center. Cinda Greely, a petite and well trimmed Chinese American who managed the center, looked at him as if he was taking her daughter out on her first date. Or worse; for the entire night. She was another hard to crack case. He'd never seen her smile; he was sure she was an autotron reject from some Disney movie that resented being separated from the rest of her form-cast siblings. Had her shinny black hair been allowed to hang down to her shoulders, she might have been fairly attractive, but with her hair pulled up in a bun and that non descriptive lab coat she looked just like any other mainframe fixture in the room. Only her light brown eyes beckoned Paul to take an occasional second glance. She was sharp too: another potential successor to his job. Had she and her experts been able to patch through, there was little doubt he would never have gained access into this restricted area. Even as director of his department his security clearance was one step below the people sitting here during normal operational times. He couldn't wait to sit down in front of a familiar keyboard and type away. Cinda Greely left the room in disgust.

Paul went straight to work trying to open a line of communication with the satellites. After a couple of hours though, a disparaging feeling swept over him. Here he was poised for greatness, and he couldn't even break into the system. General Moorehouse stopped by for a second, but only took a quick glance inside, then left. He too had become disgusted with the lack of progress and finally stopped asking for progress reports. All he could see were a large staff with not a clue as to how to get the baffle stars to respond to their commands. What good were they? He thought to himself. The fact that he understood few of their difficulties only furthered his frustrations. Only a few more hours and a rampant defense system would annihilate a Russian spacecraft. Why were they allowing it to happen? Possibly three or more cosmonauts sat in that tube. If they died so would his dreams. He would be politically dissed and become a social outcast. He already felt the stigma of being the man responsible for helping the old Soviet diehards once again regain power. He could just see the battle stars now: Altering orbits until they had destroyed everything rotating around this crazy planet. Billions spent on a program that basically stated, "If it flies, it dies." Trillions of dollars worth of orbiting technology would be wiped out within a few months. And defense? Without satellites, America would have to depend solely on ground based- out of date-radar stations for its national defense. What a throwback that would be: No time to react. All they could do would be to count the incoming missiles. Advanced missiles were just too fast for anything else. Benedict Arnold hadn't damaged the country's military strength as much as he himself had. His joint venture with the former East Germans had failed. He thought he could use them as double agents and stay one step ahead of them. They helped get him his funding, helped him recruit his top scientists, and now because of this, his ass would end up served on a silver platter. He would be disgraced. His entire military record would be dumped and deleted. He saw the damage as already past the point of reconciliation. If the new commonwealth's cosmonauts were executed, he would take his own life. It would be the only honorable way out of all this.

Paul saw the General's reflection in his screen, but didn't turn around to greet him. There was no time for him right now. He did however; happen to notice the hazy expression on his face. His smile was gone. He looked ill. He waited a minute after the General left then pushed back his chair.

"I give up," Paul said. He was exasperated. He looked around the room at the eleven remaining co-workers. "Lets all take a break," he said as he gazed up at the tiled ceiling. It was no use he thought to himself. Tim had made it virtually impossible to break into the system. It only proved what a great computer analyst Timothy Winters had once been.

While the others stood milling around or getting another cup of coffee, a reoccurring question came back to him. It just didn't make sense. If Tim could block them from redirecting the LBS'S, and the new soviets already knew the frequency code, then why didn't they try and redirect the battle stars for their own goals? Tim could help them if he was truly alive and somewhere buried in Eastern Europe. The whole thing was baffling. It was like they had all the pieces to the puzzle, and yet held back from putting together the big picture. Only two solutions came to mind. Either the suspicious nature of the newly restructured Russian government concluded that Tim was still holding something back from them, making them reluctant to proceed, or maybe they wanted this to unfold as it had. It would give them a justifiable excuse to attack consolidate more of their former domain. Such an act could re-unify the Soviet Union. Political dissension in satellite states would be squelched. The people would be forced to rally behind inclusive military might and escalation to all out civil war would soon be imminent.

CHAPTER 26

Commander, Lieutenant Colonel, Yuri Gregorovich of the renamed commonwealth space shuttle, Buran, waited patiently for new orders. The improved computers controlled every aspect of the flight and he was left with little to occupy his time. For co-pilot Major Pyotr Konstantine the strain of having no purpose or set goal in mind was worse than a routine flight. Their present role was indicative of what their ground staff constantly expressed amongst themselves. They could have sent it up without men on board. A chimpanzee could have commanded this flight Yuri thought. A chimp's only task would be to see that the human crew was fed according to schedule. Meaning, there was nothing the humans could do that the computers couldn't do. Sure they were told during briefing that if it came down to it, and something happened to the Russian version of mission control, they would have to destroy the American Satellites. But they could only do that, if their comrade scientists were correct in their assumptions: American Laser based satellites were not as indestructible as the Americans claimed. They were not armed as heavily as reported, and finally, that their computers were unreliable from overwork and unable to cope with the amount of data that had to be ingested before any reaction could be expected. None of this had anything to do with why they were up here. They were here for the effects of flesh and blood. He knew before lift off that the loss of electrical equipment or the orbiting debris of a defunct spacecraft could not stir a nation. What was needed was loss of life and limb of one or more drummed up public heroes; two town boys whose deaths would create a national rally against their aggressors. That was why they were here. The commander wouldn't admit it, but facts were facts.

"Commander, how much time do we have left?"

"You make it sound as if it is us who will loose this confrontation. I meant no disrespect."

"Your a pessimist, Major. How did you get assigned to this mission?"

"I'm pragmatic not pessimistic. That's what makes me the best weapon's officer and your present companion." If any other man had said this, Lt-Colonel Gregorovich would have deemed him a braggart, but not Pyotr. He was the best, and he was glad to have him on board. Secretly he too felt the ineptitude of their position, but as commander, he had to retain confidence. They were told before lift off that they might be required to destroy the Death Stars, but only on command. They of course could fire in self-defense at anytime, but who really wanted that option? General Vasili Kerchenko would be the man to instruct them when to initiate attack. He of course was old school GRU. He was a powerful man in the new Russia, and a firm believer in Military might. It was said that he had a hair follicle for every man killed under his command during the Afghanistan conflict. His stoic gray beard was thick, but close shaven. Whether the accusation was true or not, was not important. To play it safe was the name of the game. Yuri did not want to be named in honor of the stubble encroaching around the General's cheekbones.

"Commander Gregorovich to control, position check." He didn't have to ask; his onboard computers though simpler than the American versions, were working flawlessly. He just needed to hear Kerchenko's voice; a confirmation by radio link that they were both rational and in the same real world that seemed to be going down hill fast.

"General Kerchenko to Yuri, over. You are in orbit 174 by 168 after your last scheduled firing. Your inclination is 51.6 degrees. You are doing fine comrade. Major Konstantine maintain readiness. We hope the American aggressors will heed our warnings and your skill will not be required." Pyotr knew what he meant by this. In case the channel wasn't secured, the Americans would hear a warning. At the same time it was aimed at Pyotr's earlier pessimistic statement. What did it matter if he sounded a bit unpatriotic? Within a very short time he would either be a hero for destroying the American runaway death stars, or be known as one of the first human casualties of America's white elephant. One hit by a well-aimed smart rock could reduce his shuttle to an orbiting funeral parlor. He was damned if he would let that happen. He re-checked his control status. He would have liked to confer with Yuri in private, by slate board, but the cumbersome suit made it too difficult to do. The fact that they even had to wear the gangly outfits was a testimony to their current situation. As if you read his mind he said:

"I can't wait to get out of these suits and back into blue jeans." He almost slipped and said 'American blue jeans', but caught himself at the last moment. How could their new American friends do this to them? How could they put themselves in this current situation? He couldn't see the smile hidden behind Pyotr's helmet visor, but he knew it must be there. He took a sip on his water hose and mentally went over his evasive maneuvers.

"Cabin pressure is 1.12 kg/cm squared. Oxygen level is 23% and temperature is 22 Celsius. A nice day on the Baltic sea," Pyotr said as he too, mentally prepared himself. Both men fell silent and looked out at the round ball hued by a blue ring. The view brought on a wave of sentimentality for each of them.

CHAPTER 27

Fifteen minutes remained for the crew of the shuttle if
Houston's calculations were correct. Only the Russians themselves
could stop it now, all avenues to gain contact with the LBS's had
been exhausted. The people still gathered in the room had already
confirmed this fact amongst themselves. No one felt the urge to
come forward and make the statement official to the press. There
was still hope, if nothing else. To add to the grim scenario Susan
Chan walked into the room and flatly announced: "General
Moorehouse has just taken his life." No longer able to carry the
existing burden, he swallowed a cyanide capsule. Most likely,
people would think the pill was a relic that he had collected during
his years as a military giant and kept for the day when stress or
physical frailty robbed him of his own self-image. He had once
stated he never planned on growing old. The fact that he lived this
long was a thorn in the side of his many adversaries. His mental
problems were hushed up by the military and retirement the
antidote. He continued to be a powerful figure in the defense
industry. Meanwhile, age and related effects took a toll on his own
self-perceived image. The feeling of failure dissolved as the
capsule broke between his teeth. He had been lead down a fool's
path by foreign agents. He helped a corrupt form of government
gain a foot hold back in power. They would soon regain most of
the old Soviets territories. Worse, he inadvertently shifted control
of his Star Wars system over to them, and now they had him. A
hand written letter told the rest of the world that he was sorry for
the monstrous Pandora's box he had nurtured to life. He
apologized, signed his name with unordinary large bold strokes,
and then bit down on the pill he had been rolling around in his
mouth.

Susan had held back her feelings as long as possible.

"There is something you were never told Dr. Crellin".

"And what was that?"

"Each LBSs has a separate computer controlling a small laser platform. You weren't told. You didn't have a need to know. They have pin point accuracy." She turned around and left the room. On the way out she raised several Kleenex tissues to her face. Two technicians quickly followed close behind her.

So that's why the Russians feared them so much Paul thought. The US had unilateral orbiting military superiority over every sovereign nation.

"Can I have your attention?" one of the junior analysts, John Trenton, spoke up. Being the only member with Quebec-French Canadian accent, he quickly got the rooms attention. "Everyone except for Dr. Crellin please leave the room." Before anyone could question him he shouted out again. "Everyone except for Dr. Crellin please leave the room." Paul didn't have a clue as to why the young man said this. His face drew a blank as big as everyone else's. He did note however, that all personal appeared to comply with John's request. They all walked out half stunned and dazed by the current events. Everyone that is, except for Patrick Chandler.

"Get going, John barked and glared at him.

"Give me a reason," Patrick said stubbornly. He was ticked off that an underling was trying to boss him around. His own ego took over; he had a right to be here and he would stay as long as he pleased. A moment of silence reigned then abruptly John turned and ignored him. He was after all, an irritant that could be dealt with.

"Dr. Crellin, if you could link up to the SAT's would there still be time to overt them?" Paul looked quizzically at him. The man's eye's were cold calculating brown dots like a wolf s eyes right before it attacked. He gave Paul a strong feeling of uneasiness.

"Anything's possible, but there's only a few minutes left for those cosmonauts." He wondered what the man was up to.

"Would you even have time to say . . ." he paused for a split second. "Disperse them so they weren't all concentrated over Eastern Europe?" Paul could feel the adrenaline rush through his body. The man knew more than he was letting on, but whose side was he on? Was this another risky situation or just an outright trap?

"If I could get through . . ." his throat was dry and he found it difficult to speak. There was no telling what the consequences would be. Could he hesitate any longer, or did he dare risk exposure. He coughed and felt better. "I could do it under a minute."

"What are you talking about?" Patrick demanded as he moved towards the two men. A gun appeared from inside John's lab coat pocket.

"Step over to the wall,' John said as he leveled the carbon/plastic muzzle at Patrick's face. His body froze. Stopped dead in his tracks. He slowly backed off. John slightly altered his aim, and pulled the trigger. A small popping noise echoed in the room. A bullet hit Patrick in the chest. He stared in disbelief at the crimson colored hole as he slumped to the floor. Paul rose up out of his chair in a desperate attempt to overpower John, but was stopped by the gun as it pressed into his forehead.

"That man is seriously wounded, but do you have any idea what a bullet straight through the skull will do? I know, because I've done it before. Most of the contents splatter behind the victim." Paul's shoulder muscles spasm continued uncontrollably as he tried to discern a fight or flight response. John didn't hesitate; he shoved Paul back in his chair with his free left hand.

"Send this message, the satellites will respond." A small cassette materialized from nowhere into John's hand. All Paul could really visualize was the muzzle of the black handgun.

"We're probably too late to save them!" He wondered why the man hadn't done this when there was still time.

"If they die, then we only improve our chance of obtaining world wide condemnation of your death stars." The man was probably ruthless as Stalin, Paul surmised. Without another word he reached for the tape and inserted it into an open slot. He pressed a button marked transmit then held his breath. Instantaneously, the computer responded with the words, 'Ready For Transmission', printed across several surrounding monitors.

"Please hand back the tape," John ordered. Paul did as he was told. He watched as the man put the tape in a small plastic bag filled with a gel like substance. He was sure the tape's contents were instantaneously destroyed.

"This is all part of detente," John proclaimed. "We can't control it, and you can't either." Paul said nothing. He just looked at the man. "Now that that's safe, enter your orders."

Prior to this stage of events Paul thought he knew exactly what he would do. Now that the moment of truth and decisiveness had arrived, he found his reasoning skewed. He could become a major figure in a conspiracy, branded a traitor, or the savior of the cosmonauts, if there was still time. His batch file was set up to do what the Russians wanted. The logic behind their request sounded reasonable. Especially now, after what Susan Chan told him about the lasers. Why should one country have an unfair advantage over another? And how could the Americans be trusted even if they said they would share their technology? But was it right to usurp the authority of the United States government because he, one man, seemingly knew better than the elected people in power? What was that old expression anyhow? My country right or wrong? The men who died in Panama, Grenada, and the Persian Gulf didn't question their duty. Resolving the issue on his own would put him in the same political league as Jefferson Davis. No, he thought, a country is only as strong as it is unified. Self-fulfilling ideology could only fragment a great nation or destroy a poor one. He would not be Janus-faced. He could not be the man to make such a judgment. The Russians threatened with retaliatory measures, but it was not his place to solve the dilemma. It was impossible for someone in his position to get a clear picture of the overall perspective; those in the White house could. And without a complete understanding his judgment would be flawed.

"No," he said. "I can't." John became infuriated.

"You have to, you are ordered . . ."

"No." He looked at the gun then at the man's beet red face. He didn't see it coming, but he fell to the ground as the man shoved his knee up into the side of Paul's body. He fell in agony. The area around his left kidney was on fire with pain.

"Maybe you should reconsider before I feel less lenient." Just as John said this he turned his head towards the entrance as several armed people entered the room. He recognized the weapons and knew he had only time enough to fire one last shot. As if trained in this sort of behavior, he swiftly brought the gun up into his mouth and pulled the trigger. He stood standing still for a moment as two agents rushed forward. His head hit the floor and lay face to face with Paul, only inches away. Blood pored out of his mouth and out the back of his head. He died instantly. The two agents stepped over him and gently raised Paul back to his chair.

"Are you all right?" one of them queried.

"Jesus Christ," the other agent exclaimed. He turned from the sickening scene and almost became violently ill. The smell of gunpowder didn't help relieve his nausea.

"I'll be fine," Paul said as he stared at John's blank expressionless face. He looked over to Patrick, who other people wearing civilian suits were removing from the room. One of the rescue team members shouted: "He still has a pulse. We'd better hurry.

"You stood up well," one of the agents who appeared to be in charge said to Paul.

"Who are you?" Paul asked half bewildered. "CIA? Do you think you could do one more thing for us?"

"What is it?' These men undoubtedly saved his life, so within reason, he couldn't refuse them one last request.

"We want you to go ahead and do as John Trenton said." Paul just looked at him. He was absolutely dumbfounded.

"But those cosmonauts are probably already dead by now. Why?"

"Presidents orders. We make it look like they've succeeded at this end, so they can make up excuses to down play the current crisis. We know you can do it, and we also reassure you that in no way will it reflect on your patriotism." Paul never expected this vote of confidence.

"Ok, you asked for it." He pressed a few keys and his batch file hidden in the main computer archives was transmitted up to the orbiting LBS'S. He would now have to wait and monitor the effects of his handicraft. He wondered if it would truly work?

CHAPTER 28

Commander Yuri Gregorovich patiently wafted knowing full well that their orbit would soon put them on their closest approach to the American Death Star. Yuri felt every muscle in his body tense up. Give us the signal, he said to himself. Give us the signal to blast the son of a bitch out of the heavens. He knew full well that the so-called smart rocks were more than lethal. Knowing what he did, the prospect of destroying a smart rock after it had been launched seemed very minuscule. Pyotr would have a better chance at the entire laser platform than with a small, three-kilogram, object. Suddenly warning chimes rang out and Pyotr's radar screens lit up. A lone blimp made its way towards them. Instinctively, Major Pyotr Konstantine fired off three distinct laser blasts at the incoming object. With his free right hand he fired the two make shift rockets at the American platform. He had gone over the procedures for over the last hour and his actions went like clock work and faster than even, he anticipated.

"Control, were under attack. Taking evasive action." Yuri pushed the throttles and the great engines rumbled to life. The ship was preset to go up another twenty-five miles using its oversized thrusters. From there Pyotr could pot shot all day at the LBS'S. Only Pyotr didn't think it was possible to evade every inbound shot, even at that distance. Damned Americans. Only their technology kept their society from crumbling in chaos. A heavy womp sound came from his left side. The engines that just came to life, died abruptly. Strange scratching noises emanated from somewhere behind him. To tell the truth, the sound of metal being wrenched scared the hell out him.

"Control, I think we have been hit. Control we have been hit. Status report Major." There was no reply. Strapped in his suit he could barely move his head. He pulled open the buckles and removed his chest straps. He looked over and was met face to face with the slumped body of Major Konstantine. His dark visor was pulled down. Yuri reached over and lifted Pyotr's visor with his hand. Where there had once been Major Konstantine's face was now a sea of blood. His death had been quick and silent.

"Control, Major Konstantine is dead." There was no reply. He looked at his circuit board. Half the pin-lights were out or going out; a couple were fluctuating on and off. Cabin pressure was gone, but his hose was still securely fastened to the oxygen outlet port embedded in the shuttle's interior wall. He disconnected his hose, knowing that his backpack would last him six hours. He could exchange packs before the end of the hour, but what was the use? With communications lost, and his shuttle damaged, he was going nowhere very fast, and for a very long time. He unfastened himself, then released Pyotr. "Come along my pragmatic friend." Wrapping Pyotr's arms around him, he began to haul him out of the flight deck. He knew how Pyotr felt about space so he decided to take it upon himself to make sure that his last wishes were obeyed.

Yuri made his way to the cargo bay and strapped Pyotr to a wall while he donned a crude experimental jetpack. With the jetpack secured to his back, he tied a strap around Pyotes waist and connected to his own waist. Pyotr's blood stained helmet rested against Yuri's chest. With no gravity to pull down, the rest of his body stretched out and floated in every conceivable direction. Nothing about space could make a corpse appear normal. With himself still tethered to a wall, he hit an arming lever and the cargo doors began to open. The right door however, stopped halfway. There was still plenty of room to swing out around it.

"Well my friend its time to take you home." He became teary eyed as he unhooked his tether. With a slight kick for a push off, the two men left the darkened cargo bay and were met by the bright sun outside. Yuri was stunned by the beautiful view. He had walked in space before, but this was the first time he enjoyed it as a glorious work of God. Yuri Gagarin, the first man in space must have felt something like this he thought; back before space became common place. It was truly an inspiring view. He looked at the revolving planet he once called home. Its' blue coated atmosphere seemed so warm and inviting. "Let us go down to the

Odessa, comrade. No man could ask for a better burial site." With his hands firmly placed on the hand-controlled consoles, he pressed the appropriate directional buttons, and the two tethered cosmonauts began to move through space. Slowly, methodically, Yuri approached the tiny blue and white ball. This would be his most glorious journey; a very proper ending for two heroic sons of Mother Russia.

CHAPTER 29

"I'm going to miss you," Paul told his wife. They were standing near the boarding gate in the north terminal of San Francisco International Airport. Six armed plain-clothes agents stood close by. Gate 78 for the next fifteen minutes would be occupied by a government leased turboprop. One of the agents Paul recognized from the other day. He was the same agent who told him to go ahead and insert his batch file and alter the LBS program.

"I don't see why I can't take a commercial flight." Paul said to him, assuming he was in charge. The man never offered his name, and Paul didn't think he would even if he asked.

"This is all for your own safety," was all the response he ever got. Things were moving just too quickly. Only two days since all hell broke loose and already he was being summoned to report to the Pentagon. The six agents flanked him and followed his every move. The formation attracted attention rather than giving him a low profile. His wife found it an awkward arrangement too. They still had a great deal to discuss, and he had little time over the last two days to talk to her. Someone from the press approached the group and took a quick picture.

"Quite a coup you pulled off the other day," the reporter loudly announced just to make sure he had caught their attention. The entire entourage turned to face him. He quickly snapped another photo. If he was lucky, they would use it on the front page of tomorrow's edition. "I mean fixing those Lib's and saving that Russian cosmonaut.

"We still have some work to do," Paul said hoping to cut him off. The press didn't have the story right yet, but it was good news about the Russian. He had heard about it soon after he gained access to the main program. One of our own space shuttles lifted off shortly before the Soviet shuttle was attacked. Soon after reaching orbit they reported the Russian shuttle disappeared from their screen. They were given the go ahead to go find out what had happened when they came upon the debris.

Pieces of Soviet built hardware blew apart and slowly made their way back down to earth spinning in different trajectories. Mission control officer, Barry Levant, a black native Mississippian with a protruding belly, spotted a strange object heading directly towards earth farther away than the rest of the debris and traveling at an odd, yet quite specific, velocity. The shuttle crew altered their course and headed towards the curious object. Jane Rigors, a NASA crew specialist and holding a doctorate in aviation medicine, was already suited up in case they found anything worth investigating, or if worse came to worse, retrieving what was left of the Russian cosmonauts. The pre-planning came in handy when they spotted the free-failing cosmonauts. She exited the shuttle, used her jetpack to fly into the debris, and retrieved the two men.

"You're not going to believe this," She said as she approached the grisly sight. "One is definitely dead, but the other may still be alive." She maneuvered close by and looked into the faceplate. His eyes were closed. He was probably unconscious or asphyxiated. She wrapped a tethered line around his shoulders and used the thrust of her jetpack to pull them back to the shuttle. The one with the blood stained helmet she left loosely strapped in the cargo bay. It was the best she could do on short notice. Her main concern was to get the other one inside as quickly as possible. She carried his into the open hatchway and shut the door immediately.

"His oxygen supply is gone." One of her crewmates said as he entered the re-oxygenated chamber.

"Get his helmet off," Jane yelled as she tried to remove her own. The helmet came off and a portable oxygen supply mask was shoved on the cosmonauts face and strapped on tight.

"He's got pulse!" The Captain of the shuttle crew said as he leaned over the cosmonaut's body. "The crazy Ivan got out of his ship just in time, but where in the hell did he think he was going?"

"I think he planed on burning up upon reentry," Jane said as she sat back and rested her back against the wall. The adrenaline rush had left her muscles feeling tired and sore.

Instead of being martyrs, Yuri Gregorovich along with the crew that saved him were greeted as heroes back in Florida. He, along with the deceased Pyotr Konstantine, were going to fly back home in a few days. At least that's what Paul read in the newspapers. The media also mentioned scientists from Wescon Industries had stabilized the "Laser Based Satellites."

"Its time to go," one of the agents said. Paul kissed his wife one last time then passed though the door of the Jet way. He carried nothing with him but a small black brief case they gave him to use for some personal items. It was big enough for what he was carrying, because he didn't plan on staying there long. Helen watched as they shut the door to the jet way, then she went over to the big tinted window that looked down on the tarmac and the taxing planes. From here she would just be able to see the back of Paul's head as he entered the turboprop. She waited anyway, in hopes he would turn and wave with his hand, one last gesture of good by.

Paul heard the door to the jet way close behind him. "Wait right here," the agent in charge said. They had only taken a few steps in the passageway, so he wondered what they were up to. Then, looking forward he saw something that at first startled him. Two of the agents guarding him went forward and approached three men who had been waiting inside the ramps passageway. One of them wore clothes identical to Paul's, right down to the exact same style of briefcase. The man turned and Paul froze dead in this tracks. He wasn't sure what to think, but there in front of him was an exact double of himself. The man gave Paul an eerie smile as he was escorted through a ramp service door, and down the side stairs in full view of the terminal's windows. Helen waved at the figure as she watched him walk over to the stairs of the small Jet-prop plane. Paul's double turned just before boarding, smiled and waved at the dark tinted windows of the building, and then swiftly stepped inside the plane.

"You weren't suppose to do that," one of the men sitting beside Paul's double snapped at him.

"Relax, I was just giving you guys your money's worth."

The agent in charge checked his watch.

"Move the gate back," he suddenly barked. The ramp veered to one side and the front section retracted. The side stairs were swung over to blind spot next to the terminal building.

"Lets go," he said. Paul stood still and said:

"Go where? What was that all about?"

"I'll explain all of it in good time. Right now the President is waiting to meet you. Your last minute debut of defiance the other day made you a goddamn patriotic hero."

"You stood by and watched. Didn't you?" Paul said accusingly. He could only think that Patrick Chandler might have bled to death because of this man."

"We had to be sure of your loyalty."

"But you knew all along what I'd do."

"Some things have to be put to the test." It sounded like something better left in a movie than real life. The men he was dealing with were capable of anything. Only the outcome seemed to matter.

They all marched down the jet way and exited the side stairs and were swiftly ushered inside a waiting limousine parked underneath the terminal's concourse. Then, as they got inside the car the agent in charge began to relax.

"By using the 'LBS network' as a defense curtain against all nations, you've lessened the world's anxiety that we planed a first strike. On the other hand, the fact that they are up their gives the new Russian puppet government, and their resurrected army, incentive to put more of their already overburdened financial resources into their defense budget. The whole thing is kind of ironic when you think about it actually. We invest 25 billion in a program, and the spin-oft in the public sector generates some 18 trillion dollars. That's a hell of a lot of jobs and new products to make life easier. Were talking ceramics, electronics, lasers, and computers. The Russians, take the same Goddamn program, and it plunges them into economical chaos. It deprives their people of strapped tight raw materials, and puts them on the course as a third world nation. I bet their new government doesn't last a month."

"Haven't you heard, they're not communist anymore?" Paul said.

"That's just an illusion. As long as the Soviet die-hards are still alive, they'll be trying to run things from behind the scenes."

"I think your crazy," Paul said as he shook his head. It all felt like a bad dream that should have ended along with the collapse of the cold war era.

"I hope your right, now shall we get in the car?" Paul turned one last time and watched the plane taxing down the runway. Without another word, he stepped inside the car.

"As I was saying, it's only a matter of time before they're in deep political Caca. And that's the ultimate goal." The man was seething with self-satisfaction. Paul could feel his body tense and his hands began to tighten into fists. He noticed that he had been strategically placed in the back seat with one man on his right and the agent in charge on his left.

"What are you anyway?" Paul asked. The man looked at him as if he had just been caught off-guard.

"Why I'm a diplomat of course. Without the Russians and Chinese, I'd be out of a job! No potential enemies no guaranteed business!"

"Their political structure will no longer be able maintain their interests and they will be forced to revolt." Paul said sarcastically as he looked out the window. These men didn't care who revolted, just as long as there was a revolt. "So you win either way.

"That's it in a nut shell! You are a man of considerable talent."

"Karl Marx said it over a hundred years ago," Paul told him. "But I don't think he intended it to be applied, the same way you do. He meant it just to define political changes."

"That's another ironic thing don't you think? Using Karl's logic against the very society that his teachings spawned into existence? We must never let them return to communism."

"You know there's been a lot of changes in Russia." Paul pointed out. The case officer was babbling propaganda half a century old.

"And SDI is the final punch!" the case officer went on to conclude. He smiled as if he had devised this scenario all by himself.

"I'm sure this is all very intriguing, but Id rather discuss why that man took my place and where are we going."

"I was getting to that." He looked disappointed. "You see you're a very valuable man now. In fact, the Russians, Chinese, or anyone else bent on trying to dominate the world, would stop at nothing to win you over to their cause. Kidnapping wouldn't be out of the question. Which brings us to the conclusion, that as long as you're alive, your family's not safe either. But we have a solution."

"What will it cost me?" Paul could sense this weasel was up to something horrendous. The man could give the old disciples of the KGB a good run for their money. His wide hazel eyes made him appear amiable, but their wasn't a sincere bone in his body.

"You'll have to change your identity. Paul Crellin will have to die," He said it like reading off a list of household chores that had to be done. No emotion, just routine.

"That's your solution?"

"We could put your family under military guard for their own safety or until those LBS's become obsolete."

"You mean put them in prison."

"That's unconstitutional."

"I didn't know you read it?" The agent bit down on his upper lip. He didn't like being rebuked, but he knew Dr. Crellin would be persuaded in due time, and this knowledge helped him retain his composure.

"We can't take the risk of having the Russians capture you, the Chinese kidnapping your family, or anyone Indians drugging you into confession. You know too much. We could do our best to protect you, but one day, somehow, some way, I know something tragic would happen to you or your family."

"What about a witness protection program?"

"It might work against local gangsters or the Mafia, but your talking foreign powers with no scruples and everything to gain. They wouldn't hesitate to shoot every single one in your family; right in front of your face, just to get what they wanted. John Trenton is an excellent example of how well they can infiltrate."

"But if I theoretically die, how can I stay in touch with my family?' The agent pointed his thick stubby forefinger at Paul.

"The day you started messing around with those batch files of yours, was the day you said good-bye to your family. You won't be able to see or talk to anyone you previously knew. One mistake, one slip up, and your entire family could be put in great danger." Paul shook his head in disbelief and rubbed his neck. A sudden pain began to radiate in his chest. The fact that he wasn't sweating or felt clammy, reassured him that it was just the return of his old ulcer and not a heart attack.

"You got any Mylanta?" he asked holding his hand against the upper right side of his chest.

"Try one of these." The other agent handed him a tablet that he took out of his coat pocket. Paul accepted the pill and began chewing. His chest pain subsided within the first few swallows of the chalk like substance.

"These are dangerous men were talking about here; possibly GRU or some other elite club. Your family means nothing to them. You either decide to die or risk their lives." Paul sat motionless; he realized he was sweating and his skin did begin to feel clammy. "We'll set you up with a new life, job, whatever. Naturally you'll be funded so you can continue your research. We'll keep all options open."

"I don't want a face change." Paul whispered the words and felt as if he was talking in a dream.

"So grow a beard!"

"I won't tell you how I re-programmed the SATS."

"Given time we can figure that out for ourselves."

"I still don't like it."

"The request comes from The White House."

"What about Timothy Winters?" He was grasping for anything he could think of.

"What about him?"

"The Russians have him, they don't need me."

"Oh he's somewhere in the Russian Republics, but one of our sources in Moscow says they've diagnosed him as having aids. We think what really happened is they made him believe he had aids and then told him they had the only effective aids treatment. They don't of course, but they do have the solution to the virus they infected him with. They probably told him he would have to stay and undergo a lengthy treatment if he was to make a full recovery. Slickest operation they ever pulled."

"Well if they have him, then they don't need me."

"That's the problem. The Russians don't have him."

"I thought you just said he was in Russia."

"Actually, we think he's in Uzbekistan in the care of a group of reborn Soviet wanna be's." And besides not knowing exactly where he is or with whom, there is another complication. The virus they infected him is reported to be unstable and may cause some side effects. Our contacts tell us even the Russians don't know if Tim will make it." Paul's head slowly lowered. All this time he thought Tim was high on cocaine. Tim couldn't be corrupted by the five usual vices so they created a sixth. They gave him little choice to cooperate. They just forced ft upon him.

"I guess I don't have much choice either," he conceded.

"Its either total isolation from those you love, or they'll inevitably be killed. It's not a threat, just the facts." Paul drew a deep breath, held it, felt his blood pulsing through his head, exhaled, and shook his head in despair.

"Go ahead, I'll do what ever it takes to save my family."

"Then it's a done deal." The case officer pulled out a cellular phone form his coat pocket. " Proceed," was all he said. He listened for a brief second, and then hung up. The dark windowed limousine pulled out of the under-passage and headed down a maintenance access road.

"So tell me about my double ganger." Paul said. The agent shifted tactics and put on a solemn expression.

"I guess you haven't heard on the radio yet. The plane carrying the man in question, just blew up in mid-air.' Even the flight crew was killed."

"You bastard." The case officer held out his hands as if there was nothing he could have done to stop it. Paul couldn't believe the man's callousness.

"Who was he?" Paul coldly asked.

"That's the amusing part. He used to be a double agent. Thanks to Moorehouse's suicide note, we were able to piece it all together in time. We have a file on him now. Its been confirmed that he once disguised himself as an accountant while working for the KGB. You might say he even had a hand in recruiting you into the program."

"No! You're lying."

"Mr. Winters was extremely unstable. He must have once mentioned your name to the wrong people. Did you know that the man who took your place on that plane handwriting's identical to your ex-accountant's? He canceled your insurance and was instrumental in making your company to go bankrupt. His testimony was beaten out of him by a couple of rented thugs just yesterday. We taped his confession in case you needed proof. I can play it for you if you want?'

"No, that won't be necessary." The whole world seemed to be caving in on him.

"Were the pilots in on it too?"

"That's the tragic part. It seems a few innocent victims occasionally pay the ultimate price for the deeds of others. Its a good thing pilots are a dime a dozen. We rented them fairly cheaply. By now, Paul wasn't even fazed by the needless bloodshed. All he knew was that he had guaranteed his children over fifty years free from nuclear destruction and in return he had lost the right to be part of their lives. As far as he was concerned, he did die on that flight.

CHAPTER 30

Special Agent Jim Teller opened the door and heard what sounded like the pinging of a silenced .22 caliber; a perfect weapon for a sniper. No matter how many times he entered this room, he could never keep his adrenaline in balance. He was trained for combat against terrorists. His muscles were toned to kill a man with little expended energy. He was ready for anything, yet he could spend the next five years stuck in this isolated cabin turned sanctuary without a single incident. Or they could come for him within the next hour and all hell would break loose. With only three men on duty, the choice was simple. Either repel the aggressors or make sure no one got to the man they were protecting; that included taking his life if necessary. It would be a tragic waste. One he wasn't sure he could live with. He thought about it every time he began his shift, every time he came into the room, every time he checked the safety on his gun. He was told the man they protected was extremely important. He wondered how this scenario had evolved.

The old man started from the crackling noise emitted from the fire: a routine event that announced the arrival of a fresh bodyguard and the departure of the old. How long he had been asleep, he wasn't sure. He rubbed his transparent hands across his wrinkled eyes then watched as the pitch ignited, sending orange plumes from either end of the logs. Often he awoke from his catnaps to find himself mesmerized by the beautiful torrents of color. Thoughts of past exploits raced through his mind undaunted by the sporadic movements of the bodyguard as he desperately attempted to sweep up the tiny pine needles that now littered the floor. Always the same old mess, Jim thought to himself. Why did the old man insist on fresh pine? What was wrong with oak? He nimbly held the chard metal handle of the ash broom as he swept the debris into the pan. He soon detected the faint telltale signature of smoke and checked to see if the damper was all the way open. Already, the heat was killing him. And on top of that, his left hand was covered with soot and pitch. He kept his right hand clean; ready to go for his .38 caliber in case of emergency. Fortunately, he and his coworkers left a large bar of soap and a bottle corn oil next to the sink to take care of the mess. The oil removed the pitch; the soap removed the oil.

Over the last forty years the scorched black pyre kept the log cabin warmer than the old man's attendants appreciated. The main study was unbearable to all but he himself. He did this on purpose, for when his guards could no longer tolerate the heat, they would excuse themselves from his presence. He valued this period of time the most, for only then did his paranoia subside enough to dare let him pull out his secret papers and work in earnest.

Jim swept the fallen pine needles into the flames. To the old man they crackled as if they were a staccato of muffled Chinese fire crackers. With his view blocked, he quickly lost interest and instead turned his attention to the pictures on his desk. His firm pressed lips tried to give way to a smile, but the effort was in vain. His stoic appearance had not changed once in the last decade. Trying to conserve energy, he had let his emotions die years ago. Some of the pictures had turned yellow with age. Two recent ones taken with a telephoto lens with their bright contrasting colors looked out of place. Collectively, the pictures portrayed a lineal tree of a family he had never known.

Jim turned from the fire in time to see him pick up one of the antique silver framed photos. The old man's firm hands clutched the frame as if ready to break it. His veins easily visible through the pale yellow skin bulged unnaturally. It was a strange site the guard had witnessed many times over the last three years. He stared at him until the old man loosened his grip and gently set it back in its proper place. Jim wondered what it meant. The old geezer belonged in a funny farm he thought, but orders were orders. He was told that the old man was still doing vital work for the government and was to be left undisturbed. So, he fetched wood, brought the frail figure his paltry meals, and basically baby-sat him. Six professional highly trained agents guarded him around the clock and for what? Rarely if ever did he see the old man do anything other than stare at the pictures. Some national security problem he thought with contempt. However, to come outright and complain about his assignment would spell the end of his career.

"God it's hot in here," he said in a hushed voice; the same way he did over a thousand times each day.

The old man's eyes stared at the youthful woman in one of the photos. She died several years ago, but he still thought of her daily. When together, they were never that close. Not like other couples anyway. Over the years of absence however, he had grown to love the image she left behind. The image he enhanced, polished, and refined every day. He kept his mind on his goddess while the young man finished his chores. As the attendant walked past him, he turned his attention to a recent picture of two children getting out of a car.

On the guard's way out he shut the inner door to the study. The old man listened intently. A five-foot long hallway separated the inner door from the second door. It kept the study virtually sound proof. He didn't hear the outer door shut. He knew the guard would be back in a few minutes, so he continued to look at the picture. A girl, now age twelve, held the hand of her little brother. In another time or place, he would have rightfully called them his great grandchildren, but since they knew not of his existence, the point was mute. The girl looked just like her mother. The boy however, had the eyes and cheek bone structure that spanned over five generations. He wondered what mayhem lay hidden behind those dark brown eyes. He finally gave in and smiled for a brief moment then went sullen. The sound of the guard brought him back to the present.

"I'm sorry sir, but I forgot to bring this to you earlier." As if it really mattered, he thought. He wondered how much of the old guy's brains were left anyway. He set the morning newspaper down on the desk and paused as he glanced again at the front-page cover story. The old man looked over at the clock to see the time. It read one O'clock. He seldom knew if it was day or night. He had no overriding reason to keep track of time, so he woke and slept as he pleased. He turned towards the wall where he contemplated many years ago to put a window. Like the other walls of his study, it had become a giant bookshelf that stretched from the floor up to the ceiling. Designed to be neat and orderly, it now resembled a waste paper dumpsite. Pile upon pile of faded yellow paper pressed down on the oak boards. Some of the boards slumped and bent under the added weight. The yellowed paper gave the room an old musty atmosphere. It was an eye sore. A window would do nicely there to let some light in the dreary cell. Someday he would have to go through the mess and sort it out. Then in his mind he began to rearrange the shelves, forgetting about everything else.

"The guy in this article worked with computers." Jim said out of the blue. He was pointing to a photograph on the front cover of the newspaper. 'Did you ever meet him?" Jim abruptly became very uncomfortable. He knew It was against orders to ask questions that related to his identity, but curiosity got the better of him. Besides, what did it matter? The old man would probably die soon taking the majority of his secrets with him.

The old man looked up at him in surprise then glanced back at the fire. He wasn't sure what to say, but alas, he gave in. "I used to know a lot of people." That was as far as he would elaborate. He wondered if the guard would press the issue? And if he did? Why? Was the government still testing him?

"The article says that the last remaining-oh, what were those words? Oh yah, Star War Satellites, were reentering the earth's atmosphere and disintegrating."

"I guess they'll be anxious to get back in space?' his feeble voice spoke up. It just occurred to him how long it had been since he had actually had a conversation with another person and the process felt rather unsettling.

"Oh, they've been ready for years." Jim wondered how much the ancient relic knew of their latest progress? The old man knew of course, but he liked the young fellow and felt like prompting him to continue talking. He saw the picture on the front of the paper and stiffened apprehensively. Jim noted the reaction, but hesitated before saying anything. His expression startled Jim. For a brief second, thoughts of having to perform CPR raced through the young man's mind and another rush of adrenaline swept through his body. Fortunately the expression quickly faded: a momentary reaction to a youthful, yet familiar face staring back at him. The photo was a snapshot of Timothy Winters. Somehow the government down played his own role in the affair and there was no mention of himself on the front cover page. The picture was set next to a photo of a SDI satellite. The caption beneath the photos stated in big bold letters, 'The Dark Age is Over.' He found the implication disgusting. Just another sensationalized hype by the media. It was ludicrous the way the news treated the incident. More importantly, he wondered what impressions would be left with future generations?

"What do you think about him?" He reached his wrinkled hand out and pointed at the picture. Jim absentmindedly looked down at the old man's balding head. A few sparse silver hairs tried to cover too vast an area. It was as if he could actually see the blood pulse through the veins in his head. Maybe that was why it always caught his attention.

"Well, like most, I have mixed feelings." He paused to collect his thoughts.

Having never before been invited in a discussion with him, he desperately wanted to leave a good impression. It was more than just having someone to talk to on this lonely post, he want to find some respect for the old man. He wondered if the rumors were true that he was a treasure chest of undocumented historical facts. It could be his one chance to solve the mystery behind the man. Why did the Secret Service have to guard him anyway? The last Soviet coup fell years ago and now America had a better working relationship with Russia than they did with Germany or their poor neighbor to the north, Canada. He didn't appear to be a fugitive. Why did they have to protect him? Who would want to attack one so feeble? His past must have been colorful.

"Like most people my age," Jim started, " I have contempt for him for forcing us to boycott space exploration. On the other hand, most feel that if he hadn't interceded, mankind was headed for global destruction." He thought this sounded politically safe.

"Thank you." The old man smiled, paused for a minute, and then continued. "You seem wise for a person your age, maybe we should talk more often." Then as an after thought he added, "Perhaps this afternoon, after I've read the paper." Inside Jim felt elated, but on the outside he remained calm in appearance.

"That would be fine sir. He then turned and left the room. Out of sight, he smiled and thought how much faster the hours would pass. It would be his personal goal to learn all he could about old man. The information could prove to be quite useful in the future.

The old man picked up the paper and began to read feverishly. At the same time he made a mental note that both doors had been closed. It was now safe to work, if only he could muster enough energy.

Paul Crellin sat at his desk reminiscing his past. He looked into the flames of the fire then back at his alarm clock sifting on his desk. It was solar rechargeable. He thought about the many breakthroughs over the years. His friends at NASA said a solar cell at first cost them $150 dollars per watt. By the early eighties if had been reduced to $100 dollars. Now it was cheaper than fossil fuel. Technology had come a long way.

The spin-oft derived from the SDI program in ceramics alone had reshaped the auto and airline industry. Artificial intelligence first applied in the Star Wars program was just now having an impact on the family home. So many wonderful things had happened, and now they could even go back in space. The main program was so flawed they could never get them to do what they wanted, but LBS's remained as sentinels destroying anything that left earth's atmosphere. The Soviet die-hards never were able to regain power. Even major political reforms in China had been accomplished. Maybe, apart from his own life, it had all been worth it.

"Doctor, I have a message for you," the young man burst in the room and announced. He actually came in casually, but Paul had slowed down with age and his perception of time was not what it once was.

"Set it on the desk," It was easier to pick up this way. His hand extended in mid-air had a tendency to shake uncontrollably. Jim set the message down and then went over and stoked the fire. Paul picked up the folded piece of paper and read:

"Sir? Recently a German extremist revealed the knowledge of your location and existence. We don't know how they found out, but we do know they had retained this information in confidence for a considerable number of years. In light of this and other developments, we see no reason to suppress your identity any longer. If you wish to return to public life, we will make all arrangements necessary. We thank you for your service to your country. I wish we knew about this earlier." The President of the United States signed it. Paul did not know him personally. The last twenty years had been an enigma. He was eighty-four now, but he couldn't remember exactly. He looked back at the picture. He was curious as to how old the little girl truly was. He speculated on whether the little boy had become a man yet. He would like to meet them he thought to himself. And above all, he wondered if they liked peanut butter and macaroni? His voice was choked by emotion:

"Young man, you and I are taking a journey," he said with teary eyes.

It was during this time that he confided in me the events that shaped his life and I wrote then down as best as I could. He died shortly after his family reunion: a proud grandfather and an unknown patriot of his country.

THE END